North Shore Baby: *A Field Guide for Parents North of Boston*

North Shore Baby: *A Field Guide for Parents North of Boston*

Dana Rousmaniere

Union Park Press • Boston & Wellesley

Union Park Press
Wellesley, MA 02481
www.unionparkpress.com

Printed in USA
First Edition

© 2011 Union Park Press, LLC
Illustrations on pages 12, 25, 32, 42,
67, 69, 77, 79, 120, 131, 163, 165, 196,
203, 216, 224, 227 © Rachel Hirsh.
Illustrations on pages iii, 41, 64, 87, 89, 111, 117,
126, 145, 150, 154, 159, 212 © Holly Gordon.

Chapter 8 originally published in
Boston Baby: A Field Guide for Urban
Parents. ©2010 Union Park Press

Library of Congress Control Number: 2011930331
ISBN: 1-934598-07-0; 978-1-934598-07-8
Template designed by Elizabeth Lawrence
Book and cover design by Holly Gordon

Although the author and Union Park Press
have taken all reasonable care in preparing
this book, we make no warranty about the
accuracy and completeness of its content
and, to the maximum extent permitted,
disclaim all liability arising from its use.

All information in this book was accurate at the
time of publication but is subject to change.

**Union Park Press titles are also available in a
variety of digital formats. Please visit our website to learn more: www.unionparkpress.com.**

Contents

Introduction

The first time my husband and I laid eyes on Boston's North Shore, we fell in love all over again. As newlyweds who'd recently moved to Boston, we took a drive north to visit a friend and never left. We knew it was where we wanted to put down roots and raise our family.

There's much to love about the North Shore, and we are hardly alone in our immediate sense of connection to this region. The North Shore has long been a source of inspiration for painters, poets, writers, and musicians, from the likes of Nathaniel Hawthorne, Robert Frost, John Updike, and Edward Hopper to countless other undiscovered talents. A tour of the North Shore will show you New England at its most quintessential, with its rocky coastlines, lighthouses, rambling historic homes, and breathtaking pastoral scenes, many of which gained international recognition when Robert Frost published his second book of poems, entitled *North of Boston* (1914).

Often referred to as Boston's Gold Coast because of its affluent seaside communities, the North Shore has long been a summer vacation destination for wealthy Bostonians and New Yorkers (or, as locals like to call them, the "Summah People"), who flock to the mansions and cottages that dot its rocky shores. But year-round residents will tell you that there's much more to the region. From salt-of-the-earth Gloucester, America's first fishing town and oldest seaport, to Salem, America's Witch City; from the historic mill town of Lawrence to Andover's prestigious schools—the North Shore offers culture, history, and the great outdoors. If you're looking for upscale restaurants and casual clam shacks, salt marshes, sand dunes, castles, camping, festivals, and farmers' markets—**not to mention** a wealth of outdoor activities—you've found your home.

Whether you're a recent transplant or a lifelong resident of the North Shore, you're bound to need a road map of the region when you're viewing it from a new parent's perspective. This book is your field guide when you're dealing with questions like how to find a lactation consultant, where to send your child to preschool, or what in the world to do when it's below freezing and there's a serious case of cabin fever cooking. It's the resource I wish I'd been handed the moment the doctor placed my firstborn, Julia, on my chest. Inside, you'll find everything from the best new-parent support groups to the most kid-friendly restaurants, from the best schools to the greatest family events offered. We've included hidden gems that have taken seasoned parents in the area years to discover on their own. Along the way, we've turned to local experts as well as veteran moms and dads who are living and breathing their own version of *North Shore Baby*. Keep a copy handy in your stroller or diaper bag, and use it to make the most of these early years together as a family. They'll be gone before we know it.

Using Your Field Guide

This book is geared toward families with children from birth to age six. We've included age recommendations where appropriate, generally defined as follows:

A All ages: Birth on up
I Infants: Birth to one year
T Toddlers: One year to two years, nine months
   (occasionally written as 2.9)
P Preschoolers: Two years, nine months and up
E Early elementary school students: Four to six years

Keep in mind that these recommendations are general guidelines and that you and the director of each activity are the ones who can best determine what's right for your child.

Geographically, the listings in this book are limited to Essex County, from Cape Ann to Greater Newburyport to Greater Salem and the Merrimack Valley. This book is not intended to be a comprehensive list of every activity you'll find on the North Shore. Instead, we've asked around, interviewing local parents around the North Shore to find "best of breed" recommendations.

See something missing from the book? Have a great tip you'd like to share? Send it to us at editorial@unionparkpress.com and we'll be sure to consider it for inclusion in a future edition of *North Shore Baby*.

1 Bringing Home Baby

Congratulations—your baby's here! (Now what?!)

WHILE IT MAY be a total cliché, it's true what they say: it takes a village to raise a family. And these days, when so many people live far away from their own families, it's not uncommon to find yourself sitting home with your new bundle of joy feeling very much alone.

Take it from me: When I had my first child, Julia, I was still fairly new in town and didn't have any friends who had babies of their own. With grandparents and other family members spread far and wide and a husband who had to head back to work after a week of paternity leave, I was on my own with the baby for some very long days. It didn't take me long to realize that I needed to find a support network. I ventured out to Beverly Hospital's MotherTalk group when Julia was just eleven days old. It was the first time I'd ever left the house with her on my own, and I was in a slight panic the entire time, trying to figure out how to get myself and a baby out the door on time, juggling the car seat, the diaper bag, the stroller—and then watching the rearview mirror in horror the entire way as my newborn's head flopped around in her car seat. (I probably drove forty-five miles an hour the entire way there—on the highway!)

But, we made it! And still to this day, I am so thankful that we did. When we arrived, we found a room full of other mothers and babies who were in the exact same boat. They'd come loaded down with their own strollers, diaper bags, and questions about how to take care of their new babies.

They were nursing and changing diapers and talking and laughing, and sometimes crying. There was an extremely supportive, knowledgeable nurse on hand to answer all of our questions and facilitate the discussion. I left feeling less alone and went back week after week without fail. It became a lifeline, and I met some amazing women in the process who are now some of my best friends.

While it's not always easy, getting out of the house with your new baby can be one of the best things you do for yourself and your baby. You don't have to go it alone. Whether you're looking for a support group, a mom-and-baby class, or simply some help with breastfeeding, newborn care, or adjusting to your new role as a parent, there are plenty of resources out there to tap into. Here, we've compiled some of the best.

New Parents Support Groups & Classes

Cape Ann

Beverly Mothers' Club
www.beverlymothersclub.com
$40 annual membership.

A Members enjoy monthly kids' events, moms' nights out, and frequent informal outings. There's also a special new moms group for those with babies under a year. It's a great way to meet other women in the area, find playgroups, and socialize. The Beverly Mothers' Club also has a Meals for New Moms program that's totally worth the price of admission.

Manchester Mothers' Club
www.manchestermothersclub.com
$40 for family annual membership.

A This 125+ member organization functions solely through volunteer efforts; it brings new moms in the Cape Ann area together for support, information, and community involvement. Annual membership in the club offers new moms access to a community newsletter, playgroups, club-sponsored events for kids and families, fun moms' night out events, and philanthropic events. The club has its own cookbook and blog. One of the best perks of membership is the Meals for New Moms program, in which members will deliver home-cooked meals to moms bringing home new babies.

Mr. Mom of New England

Action Inc., 5 Pleasant Street, Gloucester
978-282-1000 | www.actioninc.org
The group meets twice a month at Action, Inc.
Free.

A Started by single father Robert Begeal, this support group for single dads meets at Action, Inc., twice a month. The group is free and open to any father interested in attending. At each meeting, the group discusses parenting issues that dads are facing and wish to discuss as a group.

Wellspring Cape Ann Families

28 Emerson Avenue, Gloucester
978-281-3558 | www.wellspringhouse.org
Free.

A Wellspring offers a variety of free parent support and education groups that meet throughout the year. Past participants talk about how they felt connected to other members while involved in this group. Visit the website or call for current class offerings.

Greater Newburyport

Anna Jaques Hospital Breastfeeding Support Group

978-463-1079 | www.ajh.org; Search: Breastfeeding Support
Newburyport: Tuesdays, 10AM–11:45AM, Higgins Conference Room, Anna Jaques Hospital.
Haverhill: Thursdays, 10:30AM–noon, Children's Health Care, Central Plaza, Water Street.
Free.

I This breastfeeding support group meets every week in Haverhill and Newburyport. No pre-registration is required, and you can even drop in while a group meeting is in progress (because we all know how hard it is to get out the door on time with a new baby!). There's also a separate parenting support group on Wednesdays from 9:30AM to 11:30AM, as well as a group for dads called Rookie Season, which meets the first Saturday of each month.

Birth to Three
15 Market Street, Suite 4, Ipswich
978-412-0123 | www.birthtothreeipswich.org
See website for classes and open playtimes.
Free for Ipswich residents; $5 per Open Play for non-Ipswich residents or $40 per child for eight-week playgroup; $30 per child for six-week playgroup.

I **T** The Birth to Three Family Center offers parenting classes, support groups, and opportunities to get out with your child and socialize with other parents. Programs include evening story times, family fun days, messy art, and music and movement classes. Working parent Saturday playgroups are offered, as well as playgroups for parents of multiples. All programs are open to Ipswich parents, and many are open to parents from neighboring towns.

Newburyport Mothers' Club
PO Box 316, Newburyport
www.newburyportmothers.com
$45 annual membership.

A The Newburyport Mothers' Club is an organization with more than seven hundred members, offering playgroups, events for kids and moms, and a newsletter with a comprehensive calendar of club-sponsored and local events, plus articles written by members. Annual membership includes access to the newsletter, a list of babysitters, and a social networking site—plus playgroups, events, parties, outings, and community outreach programs. They also have a meal delivery program for moms with newborns.

New Mother's Support Group
Amesbury Health Center, Carriage Room, 24 Morrill Place, Amesbury
978-463-1060 | www.ajh.org/events/supgroups.html

When you have a new baby, it feels like you can sometimes go for days without talking to another adult human being. But, making connections and building a support group is so important for new moms. Studies have shown that, especially for those who may be prone to postpartum depression, the more you can touch base with other people, the better you'll feel. Peg Moline, Editor-in-Chief of *Fit Pregnancy* magazine, offers these tips on seeking out and building your own support network:

1. If you're reading this while you're still pregnant, start making connections with other moms now. This is the best time to do it, because you actually have the *time*.

2. One of the best ways to build a support network is through your childbirth class. Take people's phone numbers and e-mails and stay in touch, because these women will be the perfect people for you to hang out with later—you'll have babies around the same age and be going through the same things at the same time. No one will be more sympathetic to what you're going through than another mom.

3. Try to connect with an older woman who's been a mother, who has a little more experience, and who loves babies. Most of us don't live near our own mothers anymore, and this is sometimes even better than having your own mother around to help, because there's no judgment and no emotional baggage.

4. Cultivate a friendship with a neighbor so you don't have to get in the car or travel very far to find help.

5. Lactation shops and lactation groups are a great place to meet moms. There's something very soothing about nursing and something about nursing in a group that makes you really feel like you're part of a tribe. It's something we don't experience much in our culture anymore, and there's something very primal and reassuring about being able to sit around and talk, find the comfort of other moms, swap tips on baby care, and just chill out and nurse. That's really worth seeking out.

6. As soon as you can get out of the house and go to a park, go—and don't be shy. There's no better ice breaker than a baby, and it's surprisingly easy to make friends when you have babies about the same age. The women you meet now will be there with you as your babies grow. They'll become your tribe.

Wednesdays, 9:30AM–11:30AM.
Free.

I New moms meet to talk about the wonder and worries of motherhood during their babies' first years, as well as to exchange ideas and information about newborn care. The group is facilitated by a registered nurse.

Greater Salem

BREAST Connection at Beverly Hospital
85 Herrick Street, Beverly
978-922-3000, ext. 2203 | www.beverlyhospital.org
Tuesdays, 8:30AM–10AM.
$10 per consultation.

I This breastfeeding support group is facilitated by a certified lactation consultant. You don't need to have delivered your baby at Beverly Hospital—the group is open to any new mother needing extra support for breastfeeding or who would like to have her baby weighed. No registration is required. The $10 fee covers a consultation with the lactation consultant as well as the MotherTalk support group that follows from 10AM to noon.

The Family Network, Inc.
136 Essex Street, South Hamilton
978-468-1198 | www.familynetworkinc.org
Free.

A The Family Network offers workshops that teach basic parenting skills, such as listening, positive discipline, building self-esteem from infancy through adulthood, and more. Free workshops sponsored by the Hamilton-Wenham Early Childhood Partners.

Hamilton-Wenham Mothers' Club
www.hwmothersclub.com
$40 annual dues.

A The Hamilton-Wenham Mothers' Club has been in existence for more than ninety years! The group hosts kids' events, playgroups, and moms' nights out to foster friendship and support. The group also works to give back to the community and offers a Meals for Moms program.

Hip Baby Gear
80 Washington Street, Marblehead
781-631-5556 | www.hipbabygear.com
Monday–Saturday, 10AM–5PM; Sundays, noon–5PM.

194 Cabot Street, Beverly
978-969-3521| www.hipbabygear.com
Wednesday-Thursday, 11AM–3PM; Friday, 11AM-4PM; Saturdays, 10AM-5PM; Sundays, noon–4PM.
Free.

ⓘ Marblehead and Beverly moms say that this shop is a great place to meet new moms. The store hosts playgoups for a variety of ages, and moms are welcome to bring their morning coffee and pastries into the store!

Holistic Moms Network, Essex County Chapter
Meets at Green Tea Yoga, 7 Colonial Road, Salem
877-HOL-MOMS | www.holisticmoms.org; Search: Boston North Shore
Meets on the third Tuesday of each month, 7PM.
$45 annual membership.

Ⓐ The Holistic Moms Network is a nation-wide non-profit support and discussion group. Get connected with other moms and dads who are interested in learning more about parenting from a natural and holistic point of view.

MotherTalk at Beverly Hospital
85 Herrick Street, Beverly
978-922-3000, ext. 2203 | www.beverlyhospital.org
Tuesdays, 10AM–noon.
$5 per visit.

ⓘ This support group saved me when I had my first baby. It's a great place to meet new moms in the area, find answers to questions about baby care, and find encouragement and support in what can be an isolating time of life. The group meets every Tuesday. No reservations are required. Just drop in with your baby and join other new moms as they discuss everything from breastfeeding to bottle feeding and sleep deprivation to sex after baby. The group is facilitated by a lactation consultant, but you don't need to be a breastfeeding mother to join in. There's also a separate breastfeeding support group that meets from 8:30AM to 10AM on Tuesdays, listed previously.

MotherTime Support Group at the North Shore Birth Center
85 Herrick Street, Beverly
978-927-7880 | www.beverlyhospital.org
Wednesdays, 10AM–noon.
Free.

ℹ The North Shore Birth Center offers a warm, comfortable environment that feels like home. Pre-registration is not required for the MotherTime Support Group—drop right in! You'll be glad you did.

North Shore Mothers of Multiples
First Church of Danvers, 41 Centre Street, Danvers
978-646-9406 | www.nsmom.org
Second Wednesday of each month, 7PM.
$30 annual membership.

ℹ This support group for moms of twins and multiples meets in the basement of the church. Expectant mothers are welcome. The group also has a monthly newsletter with information on raising multiples, plus news about meetings and exchanges of baby clothing and equipment.

North Shore Playgroup
www.groups.yahoo.com; Search: North Shore Playgroup
Free.

A This group's main focus is to offer support, friendship, and to hold play dates for children, which generally take place two Fridays a month. Children in the playgroup range from newborn to about five years old.

Parents Helping Parents

Lowell, Haverhill, and Salem. See website for locations.
978-354-2660 | www.parentshelpingparents.org
Lowell: Mondays, 5:30PM–7:30PM.
Haverhill: Wednesdays, 6:30PM–8PM.
Salem: Tuesdays, 10:30AM–noon.
Free.

A Parents Helping Parents is a free, anonymous, confidential roundtable support group for parents who are feeling overwhelmed, stressed, or isolated. The group is co-led by parents and a volunteer facilitator. No parenting problem is too big or too small for this gang. Parents come to vent their stress and get practical advice on parenting. Free child care is provided whenever possible. There's also a 24/7 parental stress line for those who need immediate help: 800-632-8188.

Parent & Tot Playgroup

Beverly Public Library, 32 Essex Street, Beverly
978-921-6062 | www.beverlypubliclibrary.org
Ten-week sessions are $60 per child; $30 for each additional child.

A This is a long-running playgroup featuring crafts, songs, and free play in an informal group setting for newborns to preschoolers, with parents and a group facilitator.

Merrimack Valley

Georgetown Mother's Group

www.americantowns.com; Search: Georgetown, MA
Free.

A This group of mothers with children from birth to about age four gets together for field trips in the local area, playgroups, a walking club, moms' nights out, and family get-togethers. No fees and loads of fun!

Holistic Moms Network, North Shore Chapter

Caron Family Chiropractic, 1005 Osgood Street, North Andover
877-HOL-MOMS | www.holisticmoms.org; Search: Boston North Shore

Second Monday of the month, 7PM.
$45 annual membership.

A The Holistic Moms Network is a nation-wide non-profit support and discussion group. Get connected with other moms and dads who are interested in learning more about parenting from a natural/holistic point of view. In addition to monthly meetings, the North Shore chapter offers moms' night out adventures, playgroup activities for kids, a Meals for Moms program, local business discounts, and volunteer projects for kids.

The First Two Weeks with a Newborn

Having a baby changes everything. Learn the important basics of the first two weeks so you can more calmly adjust to and enjoy this unique time. Instructor Robin Snyder-Drummond, a certified childbirth educator, doula, and lactation consultant, works with families before, during, and after childbirth. Classes about the first two weeks are held at the Beverly Senior Center ($25 per person or $35 per couple).

Find out more at www.birthready.com.

The Mother Connection (TMC)
PO Box 4059, Ballardvale Station, Andover
978-470-1500 | www.themotherconnection.org
Dues are $29 for one year; $49 for two years.

A This is a phenomenal resource for new moms in the Merrimack Valley, with an active community boasting nearly one thousand members. TMC offers a newsletter, activities and events for families, support groups for moms, playgroup matching, workshops, seasonal parties, and much more.

Parents Helping Parents
Lowell, Haverhill, and Salem
978-354-2660 | www.parentshelpingparents.org
Free.

See listing under *Greater Salem.*

Doctors agree that breast milk is the best protection for your baby for the first six months. If you plan to breastfeed, here's how to get off on the right foot:

1. Nurse within an hour after delivery.
2. Have as much skin to skin contact as possible.
3. Keep your baby with you in the hospital so you can nurse on demand.
4. Nurse frequently: eight to twelve times daily.
5. Try to wait one month before pumping and bottle feeding your baby.
6. Seek help from a lactation consultant if you're having difficulties.
7. Connect with breastfeeding support groups.

—Joanne Huggett RN, IBCLC, Beverly Hospital Lactation Services

To find additional lactation consultants in your area, visit Breastfeeding.com's Lactation Consultant Directory at www.breastfeeding.com.

Lactation Consultants

La Leche League

Andover, Beverly, Gloucester, Danvers, Hamilton, Lawrence, Newburyport, and Topsfield. See website for location details.
877-452-5324 | www.llleus.org; Search: Massachusetts
Free.

La Leche League breastfeeding consultants are available by phone at the numbers listed on their website. All La Leche League leaders are experienced mothers who have breastfed their own babies and are accredited by La Leche League International to help mothers with all aspects of breastfeeding.

Greater Newburyport

Anna Jaques Hospital Birth Center, Lactation Connection

25 Highland Avenue, Newburyport
978-463-1079 | www.ajh.org; Search: Lactation Connection
Appointments available Monday–Friday; call the Birth Center,
978-463-1060, or the Lactation Line, 978-463-1079.
Support groups are free. Cost of appointments is usually covered by insurance, especially in the first six weeks after delivery.

Lactation consultant Ellena Preston RN, IBCLC, offers in-hospital or by-appointment outpatient visits for mothers who are experiencing breastfeeding challenges. Support groups on Tuesdays and Thursdays are open to anyone and are a way for new moms to find breastfeeding support, which can be especially important in the first few weeks. You can use the services whether you've delivered at the hospital or not. Appointments are typically covered by insurance, but the admitting office will check with your insurance when you register to confirm that. The hospital encourages pregnant women to come to the support group before delivery to learn more about breastfeeding.

Greater Salem

Beverly Hospital Lactation Consultants

Beautiful Beginnings Lactation Center, 85 Herrick Street, Beverly
978-922-3000 | www.beverlyhospital.org
Call for an appointment; lactation consultants are
available seven days a week.
Cost is typically covered by insurance.

The Lactation Center at Beverly Hospital offers one-on-one sessions with lactation consultants, all of whom are registered nurses and are board-certified by the International Board of Lactation Consultants. You don't need to have delivered your baby at the hospital to use its services. The Lactation Center also sells breastfeeding pumps and accessories, such as breastfeeding pillows and nursing bras, at very competitive prices. Additionally, lactation consultants are available to help new moms with breastfeeding issues right before the BREAST Connection Support Group meets. (See listing under Support Groups.) The group meetings are from 8:30AM to 10AM on Tuesdays. If you go a few minutes early, you can get some extra one-on-one help for a small $10 charge, which also covers the group meeting from 10AM to noon. There's no need to make an appointment—just show up!

♛ Emergency Postpartum Help

If you or someone you know needs emergency assistance with postpartum depression, call 911, go to your nearest emergency room, or try one of the following resources:

- **Salem Hospital:** 978-741-1215
- **Beverly Hospital:** 978-922-3000
- **Addison Gilbert Hospital:** 978-283-4000
- **Anna Jaques Hospital:** 978-463-1000
- **Children at Risk Hotline:** 800-792-5200
- **North Shore Emergency Services toll-free:** 866-523-1216
- **DCF (Department of Children and Families in Cape Ann/Salem:** 978-825-3800
- **DCF (Department of Children and Families) in Lynn:** 781-477-1600

Telephone Help Lines:

- **Parents Anonymous:** 800-882-1250
- **Parental Stress Hotline voicemail:** 800-632-8188. The hotline is open twenty-four hours a day; leave a message and someone will get back to you.
- **Postpartum Support International/Postpartum Depression Warmline:** 800-944-4PPD. Leave a message and a volunteer will call you back within twenty-four hours.

Websites and Blogs:

- **www.postpartumprogress.com**
- **www.postpartumstress.com**
- **www.mothering.com**

Source: Reprinted with permission from the North Shore Postpartum Depression Task Force.

Kathy Abbott, IBCLC
978-922-4289 | www.busymomsbreastfeed.com
Please call for the cost of home and/or phone consultations.

Kathy Abbott, a certified IBCLC lactation consultant, makes home visits and does phone consultations to help mothers get through breastfeeding challenges. Visit her website to find out more about where she teaches classes and upcoming lectures.

Jodi Nichols, RN, BSN, IBCLC
The Lactation Consultant, Danvers
978-766-7003
$60 per hour for the first consultation, with a two-hour minimum.
(Usually only one consultation is needed.)

Jodi Nichols is an in-home lactation consultant serving the North Shore and Boston. Jodi does home visits to help new parents learn how to position the baby, how to establish a proper latch, how to know when your baby's full, how to maximize rest, and other pearls of wisdom! Jodi specializes in breastfeeding issues with premature babies and provides written materials for bleary-eyed parents to review after the consultation.

North Shore Medical Center
81 Highland Avenue, Salem
888-217-6455 | www.nsmc.partners.org
Fridays, 9AM–11AM, in the Lynch Conference Room.
Free.

Lactation specialists at North Shore Medical Center facilitate a free drop-in breastfeeding support group for breastfeeding moms and babies. New and experienced moms are welcome.

With four locations in the Boston area (and more on the way!), Isis Parenting is a rich resource, offering numerous classes and support groups. Great Beginnings, for first-time moms and infants up to ten weeks, is one of their core classes and is immensely popular. President and CEO Johanna McChesney weighs in on why getting out of the house and making connections is vital.

"New parenthood is not easy. Having a baby can be very isolating. People live away from traditional support these days, and you don't have a Rolodex of people who just had a baby," says McChesney, who calls the new moms groups an instant community. "The support is unbelievable. It's very emotional. You see nine other people going through the same thing. You don't have to be intimidated to breastfeed or let your flabby belly hang out."

Her tips for having a successful group: "Open up and welcome these new people in your life. Share your stories. Don't be judgmental. And don't worry about germs!"

For more about Isis Parenting, visit www.isisparenting.com.

Merrimack Valley

Andover Lactation
978-494-0121 | www.andoverlactation.com
Free phone consultations up to thirty minutes; $80 visits;
$40 follow-up visits; $20 for half-hour follow-up.

Eve LaRochelle, IBCLC, RLC, has been working with breastfeeding mothers and their babies since 2003, offering support and solutions for breastfeeding challenges. Through home visits and phone consultations, Andover Lactation serves the entire North Shore area. Phone consultations up to thirty minutes are free. If you require more extensive coaching, longer consultations cost $80 and are usually completed in approximately two to three hours. (Shorter visits are prorated.) All home visits are made within forty-eight hours of calling.

Donna M. Norris, BS, RN, IBCLC

10 Dartmouth Road, Andover
978-886-4498 | lacrn@comcast.net
Call to schedule an appointment.
$85 to $100 for a home visit.

Donna Norris has spent over twenty years helping mothers and babies breastfeed successfully. Her home visits are about one to two hours. In that time, she'll take a thorough history of the mother, baby, and father, taking into account the birth experience and the events leading up to her visit. She'll then observe mother and baby breastfeeding and assist as needed. When the baby is fed, Donna develops a plan for the mother, based on her goals for breastfeeding and the lifestyle situation she's in. Donna provides written instructions for following the plan. All recommendations take into account the individual situation, and all of the steps are manageable. Donna will usually have one or more follow-up phone calls with the mother to assess her progress and to tweak the plan as needed. Often, a second visit is needed to achieve the goal.

Lawrence General Hospital Lactation Support

1 General Street, Lawrence
978-683-4000 | www.lawrencegeneral.org
Cost is typically covered by insurance.

Certified lactation consultants are available while you're in the hospital or after you and the baby return home. The hospital also offers breast pump rentals for mothers who choose not to purchase one.

Night Nurses

Boston Baby Nurse

781-690-6776 | www.bostonbabynurse.com
Pricing for overnight care can be anywhere from $275 to $325 per night. An extra fee is charged for taking care of multiple babies. Discounts apply, depending upon the number of nights scheduled.

Boston Baby Nurse has nurses and baby nannies in Salem and Gloucester who are available to come to your home for sleep advice, overnight care, or just an extra set of hands. While the company does try to accommodate last-minute requests, if you anticipate that you may need help, try to book well in advance of the baby's arrival.

Postpartum Depression

Postpartum Adjustment Group at Beverly Hospital
85 Herrick Street, Beverly
Garden Conference Room, First Floor
978-922-3000, ext. 2716 | www.beverlyhospital.org
First and third Fridays of every month, 10AM–11AM.
Free.

This group is for anyone struggling with the challenges of having a new baby or depression following the birth of a baby. Pre-registration is not required, and babies are welcome.

North Shore Postpartum Depression Task Force
www.northshorepostpartumhelp.org

The North Shore Postpartum Depression Task Force brings together the practitioners, organizations, research, and best practices on the postpartum experience. The initial scope of this task force is the North Shore United Way community, including the following towns: Beverly, Manchester, Hamilton, Wenham, Ipswich, Essex, Gloucester, and Rockport. If you need to talk to someone immediately, please call the Parental Stress Hotline: 800-632-8188.

The web is a great place to find a supportive community of parents, both locally and virtually. Check out the following sites for advice, information, or just general venting!

www.bostonmamas.com
Boston Mamas offers ideas and resources for families in Boston and beyond.

www.babycenter.com
Baby Center has some of the best online communities for practically any parenting topic under the sun.

www.babble.com
Billed as a site for a new generation of parents, Babble promises to tell the truth about parenting and offers a place online to shares stories, commiserate, and celebrate the wonder (and occasional absurdity) of raising kids.

www.cafemom.com
By moms, for moms, CaféMom offers conversation, advice, friendship, and entertainment. Moms connect on shared interests, passions, challenges, and local geography. There are thousands of groups on every topic, including some of the most popular: pregnancy, raising boys, recipe swaps, photo moms, as well as marriage and relationships.

② Gearing Up for Baby

Stocking up on baby gear, clothing, furniture, toys, and food!

IT'S MIND BOGGLING how much stuff one tiny little human being can need! If you're reading this while you're pregnant, you may feel overwhelmed by registering for a baby shower. If you've already had your baby, your home has no doubt been overtaken by a mountain of gear: crib, high chair, playpen, ExerSaucer, bouncy seat, swing, baby bathtub, baby carrier, diaper bag, changing table, and bins of toys, blocks, and books. The mountains of gear are rivaled only by the mountains of laundry that you're washing and folding as your baby goes through onesies like they're going out of style.

The way you shop may change when you start a family. For one thing, you'll probably be doing a lot more of it, and parenthood at times may feel like a balance between cleaning out drawers and dashing to the store to replenish them. But other things can change too. Maybe you're looking for more budget-friendly options. Maybe having a baby has made you more conscious of shopping for environmentally friendly products. Maybe you're looking for greener, safer choices when you buy food, toys, and baby products. Or maybe you're just so strapped for time that efficiency has become the name of the game. To that end, this chapter is about shopping fast, smart, and safe for your growing family.

Great Consignment Shops and Events

Children's Drop and Shop
North Shore and Merrimack Valley consignment events
held at various locations
www.childrensdropandshop.com

A If you haven't heard of the Children's Drop and Shop, you will soon! This semi-annual week-long children's clothing consignment sales event for gently used, name brand children's clothing, furniture, and gear has become a North Shore event. The North Shore and Merrimack Valley events, held in the spring and fall, are a great way to sell all that baby gear you no longer use and have no room for, as well as a perfect place to stock up on everything from raincoats and snowsuits to ballet outfits and holiday clothes—all without breaking the piggy bank. Ten percent of profits from every event are donated to local charities, so you can feel extra good about shopping till you drop.

The Children's Orchard
Locations in Danvers, Rowley, and Newburyport
www.childrensorchard.com

75 High Street, Danvers
978-777-3355 | danvers@childrensorchard.com

1 Merrimac Street, #9, Newburyport
978-462-KIDS | newburyport@childrensorchard.com

225 Newburyport Turnpike, Rowley
978-948-6600 | rowley@childrensorchard.com

I T P One of the best stores for gently used clothing, as well as items like strollers, swings, snowsuits, and rain gear. It's also a good place to get a few extra toys during the holidays, and you can usually find some nice items for dress-up needs. (Think: holiday clothes, Halloween costumes, dance leotards, your preschooler's obsession with tiaras.)

Just Kidding

108 Bridge Street, Beverly
978-922-6543 | www.justkiddingresale.com
Tuesday–Thursday, 10AM–4PM; Friday–Saturday, 10AM–5PM.

I **T** **P** This is a great place to get a little money back by unloading the toys, clothes, and stroller that your child has outgrown. Likewise, there's also a good selection for those looking to purchase gently used items.

Kids Karousel

199 Pleasant Street, North Andover
978-685-1616 | www.kidskarousel.net
Monday–Friday, 10AM–5PM; Saturdays, 10AM–3PM; closed Sundays.

A Looking for old-fashioned toys? You've found them! Also, a tip for moms with soccer players at home: check here first for gently used town uniforms before paying full price for new ones. Inventory changes on a daily and weekly basis.

Magic Hat Thrift Shop

Marblehead Veteran's School, 217 Pleasant Street, Marblehead
781-639-3120 | See the website for most current hours of operation.

A The Marblehead community has an ongoing thrift shop in the elementary school to help raise money for the school. Parents can buy and sell clothing, sports equipment, and small furniture items.

1. Travel and shop with a running list of what to buy, sizes for each child (shoes, tops, coats, and hats), and any upcoming birthdays.

2. Buy one size up for your child. (If you are buying for the upcoming spring and your child is a 4T, buy 5T.) Clothes that are gently worn and previously washed might have been exposed to high heat and therefore may have shrunk.

3. Stick to the higher-end brands—Patagonia, Gap, Hannah Anderson, Crew Cuts, etc. The colors will stay true, and they will wear and maintain better. Buy better quality and a fewer number of items—it's better for the earth and for your storage capacity.

4. Plan ahead. Check your calendar for upcoming events such as weddings, holidays, and other special occasions. Buy a blazer, a formal dress, and shoes for these special days on consignment. This is where you will save the most money, as you won't be making a mad dash to the mall for a $100 outfit. Last-minute shopping is the deadliest kind.

5. Make sure the consignment business you are shopping from honors, studies, and investigates the current recall and lead laws. Children's Drop and Shop (see listing under *Consignment Shops*) spends countless hours making sure all products are safe and not on the recall list. We educate our consignors on what is safe, healthy, and non-toxic.

6. If toys are at the top of your shopping list, bring your own batteries to try them out. Just because it's not working in the store or at the event does not mean that it's broken. A screwdriver and a small stash of batteries will allow you to double check the toys you are about to purchase.

7. Make a mental check list: look for stains and check zippers, clasps, and buttons.

8. Don't forget to buy basic play clothes and back-up clothes for camps, schools, and grandparents' houses. You will always need the extra sweatpants, shirts, and socks—better to buy on consignment versus pulling from your more expensive wardrobe.

—Stacey Roy Lai, co-founder of Children's Drop and Shop.

If you're looking to buy or sell used baby gear online, Craigslist for Boston's North Shore is the place to be! There are plenty of bargains to be had on everything from strollers to furniture and more. Just be sure to familiarize yourself with Craigslist warnings on avoiding recalled items, avoiding scams, and personal safety.

Boutique Baby Gear and Toyshops

Cape Ann

The Last Resort
48 Bearskin Neck, Rockport
978-546-5056
May–mid-October, daily, 10AM–9PM;
mid-October–December, weekends only.

A Great gifts for young kids, babies, and mom too! You'll find hand-knit sweaters and hats, colorful rain gear, sunhats, flip flops, and island-inspired clothes. Take those flip flops for a stroll down Bearskin Neck after you shop!

Greater Newburyport

Lively Kids
15 State Street, Newburyport
978-465-7650 | www.livelykid.com
Daily, 9AM–6PM.

I T P Inside this higher-end children's store, you'll find super cute clothes, rain boots, sunhats, sun suits, etc., plus plenty of cute onesies that say things like "Follow me on Twitter" and "I have more Facebook friends than you."

Greater Salem

Chulamama
85 Andover Street (Route 114), Danvers
978-777-1888 | www.chulamama.com

I Chulamama is a great new store in Danvers for maternity clothes, nursing gear, baby clothes, toys, and baby gear. They also have a selection of organic baby products and a price match guarantee.

Hip Baby Gear
80 Washington Street, Marblehead
781-631-5556 | www.hipbabygear.com
Monday–Saturday, 10AM–5PM; Sundays, noon–5PM.

194 Cabot Street, Beverly
978-969-3521| www.hipbabygear.com
Wednesday-Thursday, 11AM–3PM; Friday, 11AM-4PM;
Saturdays, 10AM-5PM; Sundays, noon–4PM.

Not only is this the place to meet other new moms, but it's a great place to gear up on everything from maternity and baby clothes to strollers, and sign up for some cool classes, like baby sign language or music!

Merrimack Valley

The Learning Express
4 Enon Street, Beverly
978-927-1972 | www.beverly.learningexpress-toys.com
Monday–Saturday, 9:30AM–5:30PM; Sundays, noon–5PM.

32 Park Street, Andover
978-474-0555 | www.andover.learningexpress-toys.com
Monday–Wednesday, 9:30AM–5:30PM; Thursday–Friday, 9:30AM–
8PM; Saturdays, 9:30AM–5PM; Sundays, 11AM–5PM.

A A great place for innovative, educational toys and games, as well as the classics. You'll find great activities for kids with sensory issues. Sign up for online coupons delivered to your inbox. Some stores also hold classes such as stories and art for little kids. See the websites for details.

♕ Mommies Who Shop

The Hamilton-Wenham Community House hosts occasional events for mothers to get out and enjoy an evening of wine and shopping with friends in a boutique atmosphere. Moms purchase an entrance ticket for $15 and get complimentary wine and gourmet treats, mini-spa services and beauty products, gift bags, door prizes, and raffle items. Local vendors display products targeted toward new moms with young families. Even if you choose just to browse, it's a good excuse to get out of the house and enjoy a glass of wine in the company of friends.

For more information, see www.mommieswhoshop.com.

National Chains and Discount Shops

Here are a few national chains in the area that you won't want to miss if you have young kids:

A.C. Moore
100 Independence Way, Danvers
978-750-0420 | www.acmoore.com
Monday–Saturday, 9AM–9PM; Sundays, 9:30AM–7PM.

T P Stop in for arts and crafts supplies for toddlers and preschoolers. Check the website for coupons before you go. It's also a great place to stock up on photo frames and albums for all those amazing baby photos.

Babies"R"Us
300 Andover Street, Peabody
978-532-0400 | www.babiesrus.com
See website for hours of operation, which change often.

I Babies"R"Us may become your second home when you have a new baby. You'll find yourself constantly running out for a few more onesies, some extra pacifiers, diapers, baby food, you name it. New moms will love the Mother's Room in the back of the store for nursing and changing diapers. There's also a portrait studio to snag some professional photos of the baby while you're out and about.

Baby Depot at Burlington Coat Factory
310 Andover Street, Peabody
978-531-8822 | www.burlingtoncoatfactory.com

I Located in the same shopping center as Babies"R"Us, the Baby Depot at Burlington Coat Factory has some bargains (and a smaller selection) on items like cribs, strollers, baby furniture, accessories, and clothing.

Michaels Arts and Crafts Stores
35 Independence Way, Danvers | 978-777-2526
607 Broadway, Saugus | 781-233-3111
www.michaels.com
Monday–Saturday, 9AM–9PM; Sundays, 10AM–7PM.

T **P** Another great place to stock up on arts and crafts supplies for toddlers and preschoolers. You'll also find fun wooden toys, train sets, puzzles, games, and more.

Stride Rite
Northshore Shopping Center
Routes 128 and 114, Peabody | 978-531-3770
Square One
Route 1 South, Saugus | 781-231-0756
Andover Stride Rite
27 Main Street, Andover | 978-470-3385
The Loop
90 Pleasant Valley Street, Methuen | 978-685-4311
www.striderite.com

A Check out the Stride Rite website for some great coupons before you visit one of the local stores. And for even more bargains on quality shoes, try the Stride Rite outlets in Watertown, MA and in Kittery, ME.

Spots for Green Families

Cape Ann

Common Crow Natural Health Inc.
6 Elm Street, Gloucester
978-283-1665 | www.commoncrow.com
Monday–Saturday, 8AM–8PM; Sundays, 8AM–6PM.

The Common Crow is the place to go on Cape Ann for fresh local and organic food, vitamins, herbal remedies, and homeopathy. The store has 100 percent organic produce, dairy, meats, and cheeses, plus local artisan breads and pastries baked fresh daily with organic ingredients. Soups, sandwiches, and raw-food lunches are also available for under $5.

The Green Egg
www.thegreeneggshop.com

Until recently, the Green Egg was a boutique organic toy store in Manchester-by-the-Sea. Now, it's a completely Internet-based service for organic toys and gifts, boutique-style gift baskets, hand-stitched tees, and more.

Green Life Natural Living Store
196 Main Street, Gloucester
978-283-1255 | www.commoncrow.com
Daily, 10AM–6PM.

Part of Common Crow Natural Health, the Green Life Natural Living Store sells natural living products, including books, instructional DVDs, yoga equipment, organic cotton, and fair-trade gear. Natural skin care, cosmetics, hair care, and other toiletries abound. It's also a wonderful store for buying chemical-free sippy cups and water bottles for small children.

What to do when you're out on the town and have a pooh-tas-trophe? What if you're halfway through your errands and your baby demands to be nursed? Having a few places in mind where you can comfortably plop down with the baby will make your shopping trip far more enjoyable. If you're in a shopping center or the mall, know where the baby-friendly stores are. (Think: Babies"R"Us, Baby Gap, or even a maternity clothing store.) These places always welcome moms who need a place to nurse or change a diaper and often have a comfortable Mother's Room or changing room set aside just for this purpose. The Macy's Women's Lounge at the Northshore Mall is a popular place for new moms to regroup the troops. And if all else fails, your car can be a great fallback option, especially if you have a minivan or SUV with a big tailgate or an open back seat. (Tip: Keep a separate diaper bag in your car with everything you'll need—changing pad, diapers, wipes, and a change of clothes.)

Greater Newburyport

The Natural Grocer
334 High Street, Newburyport
978-463-8713 | www.thenaturalgrocer.net

The Natural Grocer specializes in strictly certified organic produce, grown by local or regional producers when possible. The store also sells safe/ clean home products from companies that value and support their local economy and its workers through fair trade practices. Busy moms who want to serve a "homemade" meal but don't feel like cooking will love the prepared foods, which are made from scratch, using ingredients sourced from local and regional farms, whenever possible, during the growing season. Foods can be adapted to your liking if you call ahead.

Greater Salem

Main Street Market

17 Main Street, Topsfield

978-887-2005 | Facebook: Search Main Street Market

Monday–Friday, 7AM–7PM; Saturdays, 7AM–5PM.

If you were a fan of New Meadows, you're going to love its new incarnation: Main Street Market, which continues the tradition of offering great natural foods, as well as wine, cheese, beer, and baked goods—all with a charming local flair. This is the perfect spot to stop in with your kids to grab a picnic on the go, an ice cream cone, or a cup of coffee for the overworked mum! Check out their Facebook page if you want to see all the yummy goods!

Trader Joe's

300 Andover Street, Peabody | 978-977-5316

358 Broadway, Saugus | 781-231-0848

www.traderjoes.com

Daily, 8AM–9PM.

Get ready to fall in love with Trader Joe's all over again. With their devotion to fabulous labels that designate gluten-free, vegan, vegetarian, fat-free, and kosher food products, this a great place to shop if you have a child with allergies. Trader Joe's carries a variety of products that are all-natural (no artificial colors, flavors, or preservatives; no genetically modified ingredients; no MSG, and no added trans fats), but moms and dads really love it for their healthy frozen options, which make for some nutritious last-minute meals.

Wild Oats Health Food

12 West Street, Beverly

978-921-0411

Monday–Saturday, 9:30AM–6PM.

This tiny store is jam-packed with natural, organic, and eco-friendly foods and products such as supplements, herbs, drinks, snacks, and packaged foods. Although you won't find any fresh produce here, bulk bins make shopping naturally a bit more budget friendly.

Whole Foods Market

331 Paradise Road, Swampscott
781-592-2200 | www.wholefoodsmarket.com
Daily, 8AM–9PM.

If you're looking for more natural food now that you've had a baby, Whole Foods is an amazing—though pricey—place to find quality organic produce, antibiotic- and hormone-free meats, and even fish that comes directly from the Whole Foods waterfront facility at Pigeon Cove in Gloucester. You can also find all-natural baby products like diapers, sun block, and baby shampoos.

Merrimack Valley

Whole Foods Market

40 Railroad Street, Andover
978-749-6664

See listing under Greater Salem.

⟨3⟩ A Class of Your Own

Enriching things to do for you and your baby

AFTER NINE LONG months, your baby has finally arrived. It's time to get to know one another! Parent-child classes are a great way to do just that, but the many classes on offer are also a wonderful way to introduce your child to the world around them, and to meet other parents in your community.

In the early months, you may want to try music classes, sign-language classes, or mom-and-baby yoga classes. Classes such as these—that focus on the bond between infant and parent—are intimate, safe venues where you can interact closely with your child and find support from other new moms. As your baby grows and becomes more mobile and interactive, you may want to try a music or movement class. By the time your baby's a toddler, you may find yourself wanting to channel all that creative energy into an art class, or take advantage of that sponge-like brain by learning a new language together. Weekend classes are a great option for working parents—or to carve out a little special time with a preschooler or an older sibling.

During the early years, classes offer structure and schedule—and many new moms often talk about how these classes anchor their weeks in what can seem like a long stretch between weekends. Eventually, all you'll really need are some good ideas for weekday adventures. In this chapter, we want to equip you with some unique North Shore offerings that will help you make the most of this precious time together.

Of course, it probably won't be long after the birth of your baby that your focus shifts from your beautiful, growing belly to wondering if your abdominal muscles will ever come back. It's a daunting task, especially when you've just been handed a demanding full-time job in the form of a tiny and needy human being. When you're sleep deprived and exhausted by the physical demands of caring for your new bundle of joy, the thought of managing the logistics of *getting* to the gym is exhausting in and of itself. But, there are ways to make it work: fitness classes for moms and babies, gyms with child care, and other programs geared specifically toward new moms who want or need to bring the baby in tow are available all over the North Shore. We've listed just a few of the many programs out there to help you carve out a little time to take care of *you*.

No matter what you're looking for, you'll find plenty of classes, programs, and arts venues throughout the region that will keep every member of your growing family busy, engaged, and entertained for years to come!

Movement Classes

YMCA of the North Shore
Locations in Cape Ann, Beverly, Haverhill, Ipswich, Marblehead, Salem
978-922-0990 | www.northshoreymca.org
See website for gym locations and hours.

A The Y is one of the most affordable options for classes on the North Shore, with a wealth of options to choose from, including swimming, gymnastics, dance, T-ball, all sorts of adventure and sports classes, and more. The Y is also now affiliated with the Boston Ballet, offering classes at the Lynch/van Oterloo YMCA in Marblehead. The Sterling School of Dance is also a much-loved dance program in Beverly. See the website for seasonal program guides, registration dates, and even summer camps.

Cape Ann

Creative Arts Dance Conservatory

1 Scot's Way, Essex

978-922-0980 | www.creativeartsdanceconservatory.com

The registration fee for the year is $25. Classes range from $110 to $125 for eight-week sessions and are prorated if you join late.

P **E** The Creative Arts Dance Conservatory offers a variety of dance classes in a non-competitive atmosphere, including ballet, jazz, hip-hop, creative movement, lyrical, flamenco dancing, boys' movement classes (percussion instruments and dance games), and reading hour ballet (story, craft, and dance). Little girls will love the Angelina Ballerina birthday parties.

Iron Rail Mom and Me Gymnastics Classes

91 Grapevine Road, Wenham | 978-468-9544

8 Kondelin Road, Gloucester | 978-282-8855

www.ironrail.com

Mom-and-me classes are $40 per month for one class per week or $52 per month for two classes per week, plus a $40 per year registration fee.

Preschool tumbling classes are $72 per month for one class per week or $112 per month for two classes per week, plus a $40 per year registration fee.

A Iron Rail has a great facility for gymnastics and tumbling for all ages. There are some great open playgroups, mom-and-me classes (from walking to age three), and instructor-led classes for older children. Kids will love the trampolines and leaping into the foam pits. Parents will love how tuckered out the kids get. Moms and kids need to remove their shoes to play, and the facilities can be cold in the winter months, so dress accordingly.

Greater Salem

Green Tea Yoga
10 Colonial Road, Salem
978-740-9749 | www.greenteayoga.com
$75 for six-week kids' yoga sessions.

P **E** Green Tea Yoga offers yoga classes for kids as young as two years old. The classes teach kids how to increase their energy and attention, be calm, and about basic anatomy. The classes use creative movement, storytelling, and imagery. Green Tea Yoga also offers Color Me Yoga teacher training, where adults can learn to teach yoga to children. Training occurs one weekend per month for one year. The studio also hosts children's yoga birthday parties for up to ten children, age four to ten years old. Little yogis can choose from themes like circus, safari, princess, luau, under the sea, beach, magic and wizardry, and outer space.

Gymboree
64 Pulaski Street, Peabody
978-531-5420 | www.gymboreeclasses.com
Classes are generally held in the mornings, with some open gym times in the afternoons. See website for the schedule.
$69 per month. Included in every membership fee is free open gym offered a minimum of four hours a week.

I **T** **P** Gymboree has music-and-movement and arts-and-crafts classes for babies through five years. Be sure to bring the hand sanitizer, as some local moms have taken to calling this "Germboree" during cold and flu season. You can sign up for a free pass online if you'd like to try a class before forking over the credit card.

Hamilton-Wenham Community House
284 Bay Road, South Hamilton
978-468-4818 | www.communityhouse.org
See website for most current program hours and costs.

A Hamilton has a well-run recreation center that offers some very affordable classes for the community, including gymnastics, creative movement, sports jam, hockey, basketball, and soccer basics. Infants and toddlers will love Sing and Dance with the Music Man, Brian Doser, (Thursdays at 10AM; $5 donation per family), and preschoolers will go nuts for the LEGO Action class (Friday mornings at 10AM; $60 for six weeks or $15 drop-in; free demo class). There's also a Kindermusik class offered.

☀ Find Your Inner Yogi

Postpartum yoga and mom-and-me yoga is designed to nurture the bond between you and your baby; fight off the baby blues; improve your posture; and stretch and relax as you let go of all the aches and pains of the postpartum body. You'll focus on strengthening and toning abdominals and pelvic floor muscles, increasing your energy, learning relaxation techniques, and introducing yourself to a new parenting community. In addition, yoga will help your baby sleep better; assist with digestion, colic, and fussiness; increase neuro-muscular and motor development; strengthen muscles; develop social and play skills; assist babies' natural development with tummy time, crawling, and walking. Best of all, this is a wonderful way to nurture the bond between parent and child.

—Marnie Memmolo, North Shore Yoga

Little Gym of Danvers

29 Andover Street, Danvers
978-777-7977 | www.tlgdanversma.com
$40 annual family membership.

🅰 The Little Gym is great for babies, with gym classes for newborns up to about two years old (movement, dance, sports skills, etc.) and gymnastics classes for preschoolers and kindergarteners. It's a wonderful place to host a hassle-free birthday party for toddlers. Try their free introductory trial for gymnastics classes.

Mom & Baby Yoga

180-186 Cabot Street, Beverly

978-857-9063 | www.northshoreyogastudio.com
See website for most updated class times and schedules.
Session fees are $75 for four classes or you can drop in
(with a reservation) for $20.

I Bring the baby onto your yoga mat for some relaxed bonding time!
Space is limited so be sure to call ahead. Classes are for ages six
weeks to crawling.

Stroller Strides

866-FIT-4MOM | www.strollerstrides.net
See website for a schedule of classes near you.
$15 per class or $110 for ten classes.

I **T** Stroller Strides offers the perfect solution for moms who need
to get out for some fresh air and exercise with baby in tow. It's also a
great way to meet other new moms. Groups meet up in Lynch Park in
Beverly, in Masconomo Park in Manchester, and at Hip Baby Gear in
Marblehead. The group will take a fifty-minute walk together with the
babies in strollers, then stop at a playground or park to do ten minutes
of push-ups, sit-ups, and other exercises. New Stroller Strides franchises
may be popping up (and closing) all the time, so be sure to check the
website for locations. Stroller Strides recommends that babies be at
least six weeks before beginning a program.

Merrimack Valley

Andover School of Ballet

14 Park Street, Andover
978-475-5919 | www.andoverschoolofballet.com
Call to inquire about class availability and to register.
Registration fee of $15 per child or $25 per family, plus tuition
for individual classes.

T **P** **E** The Andover School of Ballet has mom-and-me dance classes
for kids from ages twenty-four to thirty-five months. Activities involve

dancing to nursery rhythms, music, and occasionally singing. Props such as balls, hoops, and scarves are also used. Come in comfortable clothing and bare feet. Early childhood programs for kids ages three to seven include Kinderdance, pre-ballet, primary, and classical ballet.

Andover Martial Arts
16 Haverhill Street, #9, Andover
978-749-0880 | www.andoverata.com
See website for class schedules and prices. First class is free!

P **E** Andover Martial Arts has classes for the entire family, from Tiny Tigers (ages three to five) to Karate for Kids (ages six to eleven) and up. Children learn courtesy, respect, discipline, confidence, and perseverance.

Boston Sports Club
307 Lowell Street, Andover
978-475-3333 | www.mysportsclubs.com
Monday–Thursday, 5AM–9PM; Fridays, 5AM–9PM;
Saturday–Sunday, 7AM–6PM.
Membership prices vary from $49 per month to $89 per month; see website for details.

A The Boston Sports Club offers recreational athletic programs for kids from six months to fifteen years. The gym also has babysitting for children from three months to ten years.

The Champion Factory
595 Chickering Road, North Andover
978-683-8493 | www.championfactory.com
See website for current class schedules and costs.

A The Champion Factory has programs for all ages, from eighteen months to middle school, offering gymnastics, tumbling, circus arts, and even juggling classes for adults! There's also an open gym time, and the center hosts birthday parties.

Dance Infusion

19 Lupine Road, Andover
978-475-7868 | www.danceinfusion.com/andoverhome.html
Classes range from $45 per month to $67 per month.

P **E** Dance Infusion has classes for ages three and four in a forty-minute tap-and-ballet combination. Classes for ages five through seven are hour-long ballet-and-tap or jazz-and-tap combination classes. Parents can pay by the month or by the semester.

Interstate Gymnastics & Dance

5 Burnham Road, Methuen
978-688-8939 | interstategymnasticsanddance.com
$80 for eight weeks.

A Interstate Gymnastics & Dance offers classes for all ages, including a mom-and-baby class that involves moving, climbing, and exploring. There's also a Sweet Beginnings class for babies three to twelve months of age, designed to encourage babies to move, crawl, and explore their world.

Master Shin Martial Art School

4 Dundee Park Drive, Andover
978-475-3133 | www.mastershin.com
Flexible class schedules are available.
The school has an introductory special that's $39 for two weeks, including uniform.

P **E** Master Shin's Little Tigers program for children ages three to five is a great introduction to Tae Kwon Do, teaching kids focus, confidence, coordination, balance, control, and discipline.

Methuen Karate Association

70 Bonanno Court, Methuen
978-683-4287 | www.methuenkarate.com
$99 for two months, including uniform.

P **E** Methuen Karate offers Tiny Tots classes (ages three to four, half hour) Saturdays at 10AM. Classes are also available for ages five and up.

North Andover School of Dance

100 Belmont Street, North Andover
978-688-6683 | www.nasdg.com
See website for class schedules and costs.

T **P** **E** The North Andover School of Dance offers preschool and kindergarten dance classes, plus kids' yoga classes for ages four through eight. Two-year-olds can take a forty-five-minute class consisting of pre-ballet, creative movement, and tap. Preschooler classes are an hour long, split equally between ballet and tap. There's also a Music Makers class focused on singing, dancing, acting, laughing, and learning.

Peace, Groove, and Happiness (PGH) Kids Yoga

Central Street, Georgetown
978-352-YOGA | www.pghkidsyoga.com
Check website for cost of individual classes and schedules.
Note: there are price breaks for enrolling in a full semester of classes.

A PGH offers an array of classes for moms and wee ones: prenatal yoga classes, mom-and-me yoga classes, and yoga for kids of all ages. The studio also has tap, jazz, ballet, lyrical, hip-hop, and Zumba classes. Get the whole family moving at this bright and energetic studio!

Ready Set Go! Inc.

126 Merrimack Street, Suite 3, Methuen
978-685-7704 | www.rsgfitness.com
See website for current class schedules and costs.

A This is a great place for parent/toddler gymnastics classes and karate classes for kids and adults too! Children learn muscle control, balance, and coordination while having fun and building self confidence. Parent participation is required. Kids three years and up can also choose from several sports clinics. Child care is available during most adult fitness classes (for children ages six months to nine years). Activity time, facilitated by a teacher, consists of movement and music, games and puzzles, bubbles, parachute games, and free play. There's also a preschool enrichment program available that's designed to be a supplement to preschool.

Music Classes

Greater Newburyport

Itsy Bitsy Music
58 Macy Street, #C, Amesbury
978-388-3773 | www.itsybitsymusic.com
Tuition is $175 per child for ten weekly forty-five-minute classes ($100 per sibling over eight months old; siblings under eight months free).

I T P Itsy Bitsy has music and arts classes for infants, toddlers, and preschoolers with parents or caregivers. Itsy Bitsy Music classes are age integrated, birth to five years, and designed with the whole family in mind. The classes maintain an informal instruction style, allowing children to participate as they choose and at their own developmental level. It's a great option for families with siblings—you can all enjoy the same class together!

The World Wide Web

A great resource for parents looking to keep their kids on the go: www.northshorekid.com.

Greater Salem

Hip Baby Gear
80 Washington Street, Marblehead
781-631-5556 | www.hipbabygear.com
Six-week class is $125 per child ($65 for additional sibling).

I Hip Baby Gear offers a forty-five-minute interactive music class that features rhythm exploration, puppets and finger play, a drum circle, a jam session, and plenty of Hip Baby singing and dancing.

Merrimack Valley

Imajine That
354 Merrimack Street, Lawrence
978-682-5338 | www.imajinethat.com
Classes are available on Tuesday and Saturday mornings.
$60, which includes a one-month membership to Imajine That playspace.

I T P Imajine That offers music and movement classes for children under twenty-four months, with their adult caregiver, and for kids ages two through four. The Imajine That programming exposes children to music through songs, games, and group activities. The classes encourage self-expression and creativity through the exploration of dance and yoga (for older children).

Kindermusik
www.kindermusik.com

I T P Kindermusik offers music and movement classes for newborns up through children age seven. During the classes, kids and their caregivers sing, dance, and play instruments. Kindermusik classes are available all over the North Shore. See the website to find your nearest location. Don't forget to download a free class coupon!

Music Together Around the Towns
197 Haggetts Pond Road, Andover
978-590-6624 | www.musictogetheraroundthetowns.com

I T P Music Together Around the Towns is for infants, toddlers, preschoolers, and the adults who love them. Classes give kids the opportunity to sing, dance, and play instruments. The classes are targeted toward families in Andover, North Andover, Topsfield, North Reading, and Newburyport.

Tiny Tunes!
93 Main Street, #16, Andover
978-475-3148 | www.tinytunesandover.com

I T P Tiny Tunes! is a live music education program that's committed to bringing music into the lives of children from infancy through age twelve. The program consists of live music classes and an after-school theater program. If you have a budding thespian at home, this is your place!

La Petite Chorale

La Petite Chorale (LPC) is a children's chorus started by Wendy Manninen, a kindergarten teacher in Manchester, over sixteen years ago. In that time, LPC has evolved from an exclusive French choir to a chorus that features a different theme each year. In years past, children have learned Broadway show tunes, country, Beatles songs, movie theme songs, and patriotic songs—which they perform with sign language. Children perform in venues around Cape Ann and Boston. Participants range in age from three to eleven years. Contact Wendy Manninen at 978-525-3911 or search online for La Petite Chorale for more information on how to get involved.

Live Theater, Art, and Other Educational Classes

Cape Ann

Cape Ann Art Haven
180B Main Street, Gloucester
978-283-3888 | www.arthaven.org
Fridays, 3:30PM–5:30PM.
$10 for first child; $5 for each additional child.

T P E Cape Ann Art Haven is a community space where artists of all ages and abilities are encouraged to develop creativity and confidence through hands on learning and collaboration. They offer a Family Open Studio for children of any age with their parents. During Open Studios, families participate in an organized art project with an instructor, followed by time to explore and experiment with all that the studio has to offer. Starting in third grade, elementary school kids can also take classes in clayworks (sculpture and collage) and art foundations (painting, drawing, color theory, composition, etc.).

Glazed!

184 Washington Street, Gloucester
978-283-5751 | www.glazedceramics.com
Tuesday–Friday, 11AM–9PM; Saturday–Sunday, 11AM– 4PM; closed Mondays.

P **E** While not a traditional art class, Glazed! offers a sunny, warm environment where kids and adults alike can get creative! This is a great place to enjoy an hour or two painting pottery. Kids will love to make their own cups and bowls safe for eating and drinking. Pieces must be picked up at a later date as they need to be fired in the oven. Glazed! also offers a summer art program, holds vacation workshops, and has a small play area in the back of the store to keep small kids occupied while they're waiting for big brothers and sisters to finish their projects.

Get Artsy!

Cape Ann Artisans Studio Tours

Take the family to visit working studios and meet the artists. See pottery, jewelry, sculpture, mosaics, paintings, photography, and more.

www.capeannartisans.com

Rocky Neck Art Colony, Gloucester

Take a walking tour of America's oldest art colony to see colorful galleries full of pottery, jewelry, sculptures, paintings, and photographs. Kids will love stopping for ice cream, and adults will love the restaurants with outdoor patios. Don't miss Nights on the Neck, featuring open studios and outdoor entertainment from 5PM to 9PM the first Thursdays of the month from June through September.

www.rockyneckartcolony.org

Greater Newburyport

TheArtRoom
30 Main Street, Topsfield
978-887-8809 | www.theartroomstudio.com
Morning and afternoon classes available.
$120 for six-week sessions; $5 sibling discount.

P **E** TheArtRoom offers classes for ages four and up in a variety of mediums and techniques each session. TheArtRoom also does birthday parties for the same age group ($20 per guest; eight to fourteen guests for a one-and-a-half hour party) that includes an art project, games, and time for cake and presents.

Firehouse Center for the Arts
Market Square, Newburyport
978-462-7336 | www.firehouse.org
See the website for current programs, schedules, and costs.

A The Firehouse Center for the Arts is an intimate theater on the waterfront in downtown Newburyport. The center offers national, regional, and local live performances at affordable prices. There's a great series for families with a broad range of family-friendly programs. Favorites include the Tanglewood Marionettes, local theater companies such as Acting Out! Studios, Duck Soup Troupe, and Theater in the Open, and a variety of touring shows that expose children and adults to world cultures, historical events, literary masterpieces, and scientific principles.

Neverland Theatre
574 Haverhill Street, Rowley
www.neverlandtheatre.com

T **P** **E** The Neverland Theatre, founded more than twenty years ago, was started to expose children and adults to the excitement and enriching experience of live musical productions. The theater produces shows that children, parents, and grandparents can enjoy together.

The Neverland also offers theater workshops and camps for kids. See the online schedule for current productions, which children of all ages can enjoy.

Theater in the Open

Maudslay State Park, Newburyport (PO Box 215)
978-465-2572 | www.theaterintheopen.org

A Theater in the Open uses puppetry, pageantry, music, and acting to transform storytelling into theater. In the summer, on the third Saturday of each month at 11AM, the theater hosts Family Hour, a free event where you can bring the kids, the dog, and a picnic blanket to enjoy storytelling, song and dance, group activities, and being outdoors. Check the website for details about Family Hour, as well as other productions, schedules, and ticket prices.

Greater Salem

Banbury Cross Children's Bookshop

162 R Main Street (Route 1A), Wenham
978-468-4040 | www.banburybooks.com
Tuesday–Friday, 10AM–5PM; Saturdays, 10AM–4PM.
Eight-week sessions, $90 for a weekly forty-five-minute class. Wee Babies and Books: four-week sessions, $50 for a weekly forty-five-minute class.

I T P This lovely children's bookstore hosts an eight-week Babies and Books program, which meets once a week for forty-five minutes, held at various locations throughout the North Shore. The class is designed to introduce babies to a love of language and a wealth of good literature. Each week includes group participation with books, stories, songs, nursery rhymes, games, lullabies, and puppetry. Themes include families, farm animals, trains, and so on. The store also offers a Big Kids and Books program for kids ages 2.6 to 3.6. All of these classes show that it's never too early to start rhyming, rocking, and reading!

Clay Dreaming Pottery Studio

186 Cabot Street, Beverly

978-927-1414 | www.claydreaming.com

Check website for various pricing options.

P **E** Clay Dreaming offers adult-and-child clay classes for parents or caregivers to learn the art of claymaking with their children ages five and up. There's also a paint-your-own pottery studio open to children of all ages. Clay Dreaming has a summer arts enrichment program for ages three to seven, where children can choose from a variety of themes in ceramics and dancing (or both!) at the Creative Arts Dance Conservatory on the premises. Themes include Fairy Tales, Bugs & Butterflies, and Disney.

Kaleidoscope Theatre, the North Shore Musical Children's Theatre

466 Central Street, Saugus

781-230-3976 | www.kaleidoscopechildrenstheatre.com

Tickets are $9 in advance; $12 the day of the show. See the website for the current production schedule.

A Kaleidoscope Theatre is a professional touring children's theater company based in Cranston, Rhode Island. The group performs children's shows around the North Shore of Boston, such as fairy tale musicals like *Beauty and the Beast*, *Snow White*, and *Aladdin*. Kaleidoscope Children's Theatre also offers several birthday party packages, all of which include a fairy tale character visiting your child's birthday party.

Kids to College at North Shore Community College

1 Ferncroft Road in Danvers and 300 Broad Street in Lynn

978-236-1232 | www.northshore.edu

$99 per course for a five-week session.

E Starting in kindergarten, kids can take Saturday morning classes at North Shore Community College as part of their Kids to College program. Class options are seemingly endless: Animal Care, Play Acting, Culinary Adventures, Fairy and Wizard House Construction, How Do

Things Work?, Painting, Young Science Explorers, Readings from Nature, Let's Play Exercises, and more. Registration is required. Sign up and let your little one be the big man on campus!

Lynn Arts

25 Exchange Street, Lynn
781-598-5244 | www.lynnarts.org
Sessions are held during February and April vacation weeks and for two weeks in July and August, Monday–Friday, 9AM–3PM.
Classes range from $150 to $175 for the week.

E Lynn Arts is a private, non-profit organization dedicated to promoting cultural activity in the city of Lynn. The center currently offers affordable, week-long art exploration programs for children starting at age six. Each week offers children the opportunity to explore a variety of visual and performing arts forms with activities ranging from puppet-making, print-making, painting, drawing, and mask-making to improvisational games, dance, script-writing, costume and prop design, and more. Each session culminates with a short performance and art exhibition.

Marblehead Little Theater

Nelson Aldrich Performing Arts Center, Marblehead Veterans Middle School, 217 Pleasant Street, Marblehead
781-631-9697 | www.mltlive.org
See website for program and class schedules.

P E The Marblehead Little Theater presents at least one musical production per year and offers theater classes for children as young as four years old. In Drama with Debbie, ages four through six, children are encouraged to use acting as a way to express ideas and feelings. The Little Theater gives children ages five to seven the chance to become little players—and the session culminates with a short play performed for their adoring audience (of parents).

North of Boston Arts Center

North of Boston Arts Center, Beverly
662-228-0033 | www.thenobac.org

Monday–Thursday, 4PM–6PM.
Classes range from $50 to $150 per month.

T **P** **E** North of Boston Arts Center (NOBAC) is a multi-media program where children of all ages can explore the world through the arts. NOBAC is dedicated to providing knowledge and education of art, music, dance, photography, multi-media, and theater culture through stage experience. NOBAC offers after-school art programs for kids starting at age five, with classes in music, health and fitness, drawing, live performance, theater, print making, puppetry, paper crafts, and more. The center also has a new Twinkle Tweets program (Fridays, 10AM–11AM) for preschoolers to create weekly operettas from children's storybooks. Now that's something to sing about!

Baby Sign Language

Hip Baby Gear in Marblehead offers Sign, Say & Play™, a six-week Baby Signs® play class (forty-five minutes long) with games, songs, and activities designed to introduce families to baby sign language. $125 (includes course materials) for a six-week class. Call Hip Baby Gear for more information: 781-631-5556, or visit their website: www.hipbabygear.com

---

North Shore Music Theater
62 Dunham Road, #1, Beverly
978-232-7200 | www.nsmt.org

A The North Shore Music Theater provides wonderful professional shows for children. The small theater-in-the-round setting gives even the smallest kids a great view of the stage. See the website for current productions and prices.

Plaster Fun Time
400 Highland Avenue, Salem
978-745-7788 | www.plasterfuntime.com
Monday–Friday, 11AM–7PM; Saturdays, 10AM–7PM; Sundays, noon–6PM.

T **P** **E** Voted as a best place for birthday parties by the Boston

Parents Paper, Plaster Fun Time is a great idea for some spur-of-the-moment creative fun. Kids as young as three will find plenty of fun items to paint—often including themselves! There's also an online club for coupons and discounts. Walk-ins always welcome.

Merrimack Valley

Essex Art Center
56 Island Street, Lawrence
978-685-2343 | www.essexartcenter.com
Monday–Friday, 10AM–6PM.
Classes start at $55 on up, for eleven-week sessions.

P **E** The Essex Art Center is a non-profit art organization that has art and theater classes for ages three to adult. Kids can explore drawing, painting, clay sculpting, photography, and more. Due to their non-profit status, classes often cost 50 percent less than other options. Register early as class sizes are small.

Imajine That
354 Merrimack Street, Lawrence
978-682-5338 | www.imajinethat.com
Fridays, 9:30AM–10:15AM.

$70 for a five-week semester (includes a one month membership to Imajine That playspace).

P Imajine That has a preschool theater class (ages three to six) where children listen to stories and bring those tales to life through guided drama and creative play. Children may use the provided props and may choose to dress up in costumes to enhance their imagination and play experience. All classes begin with a drama game warm-up to build on each child's trust and confidence and will create an environment of comfort and fun. Classes end in a calming circle time where each child receives a star stamp and a take-home creative arts page.

Kaleidoscope

Located at the Pike School, 34 Sunset Rock Road, Andover
978-475-1422 | www.kaleidoscopekids.com
See website for current programs, schedules, and costs.

P **E** Kaleidoscope is a non-profit enrichment program that offers varied educational and cultural opportunities to children in the Merrimack Valley. In the summer, Kaleidoscope offers one-week courses, where students are immersed in the subjects of their choice. Kids as young as three years old can take classes such as Seuss on the Loose, Understanding Animals, Lego Mania, Sketchbook Skills, Kitchen Chemistry, Magic School Bus Adventures, and dozens of other options.

Gyms with Child Care

Beverly Athletic Club

7 Reservoir Road, Beverly
978-927-0920 | www.beverlyathletic.com

A The Beverly Athletic Club provides a safe, well-maintained, and fun child care environment for children whose parents are utilizing the club's services and programs, which includes indoor and outdoor pools, Pilates and spinning studios, programs and classes for kids and adults, plus a private women-only fitness studio. The club offers a free trial if you'd like to check it out before joining.

Latitude Sports Club
Locations in Methuen, Peabody, Andover, Bradford, and Salisbury
888-552-8488 | www.latitudesportsclubs.com

A Latitude Sports Clubs offer the total package: everything from an indoor track and pools to a spa to a fabulous juice bar to a women-only workout center. Non-members can get a day pass to take the kids for family swim, and members can use the playcare facilities to work out while the kids play.

YMCA of the North Shore
Locations in Cape Ann, Beverly, Haverhill, Ipswich, Marblehead, Salem
978-922-0990 | www.northshoreymca.org
See website for gym locations and hours.

A You can't beat a Y membership to keep your family, and your budget, in shape. A membership to the YMCA of the North Shore gives you access to any Y location on the North Shore. The Y offers drop-in child care, indoor and outdoor pools, flexible summer memberships, classes for kids and adults, and summer and school vacation camps. Parents rave about the facilities at the Sterling Center in Beverly and the new facility in Marblehead.

Cape Ann

Manchester Athletic Club (MAC)
8 Atwater Avenue, Manchester-by-the-Sea
978-526-8900 | www.manchesterathleticclub.com

A For a monthly fee, child care is available for up to two hours a day, seven days a week. Reservations are required. The child care room is secure and clean, with a separate area for babies, an arts-and-crafts room, a toddler room, and gym jam room. The MAC also has indoor and outdoor pools, tennis courts, a spa, a café, a pro shop, and plenty of camps, classes, and activities for kids and adults alike.

Greater Newburyport

Fuel
75 Merrimac Street, Newburyport
978-463-3226 | fueltrainingstudio.com

While they don't offer child care yet, Fuel is very popular with Newburyport moms because of their cool outdoor classes, which take place on the boardwalk along the Newburyport waterfront. You can literally watch the sun rise and set as you take a bootcamp class or have a private training session. There's also an indoor training studio. Yes, you need to enlist dad's help or hire a babysitter first, but you'll love the chance to get outside and enjoy a little female camaraderie.

Greater Salem

Salem Healthworks
84 Highland Avenue, Salem
978-745-7390 | www.healthworksfitness.com
See website for hours, which vary by season.
There are a variety of membership options available; see website for details.

Salem Healthworks is the perfect gym for new moms. The nursery provides on-site child care for children six weeks to eight years old, for up to two and a half hours. (The website has online reservations for the nursery, to make your trip to the gym that much more convenient.) The gym offers state-of-the-art equipment, clean locker rooms, more than one hundred group exercise classes each week, spa services, a café and juice bar, and more.

When you live on the North Shore, you're always surrounded by natural beauty—but here are two suggestions for incorporating nature exploration into your children's lives in a more formal way.

Ipswich River Wildlife Sanctuary

87 Perkins Row, Topsfield

978-887-9264 | www.massaudubon.org; Search Ipswich River

Ipswich River, Mass Audubon's largest sanctuary, offers more than ten miles of interconnecting trails that invite you to explore the forests, meadows, and wetlands. Programs are offered throughout the year—in the summer there are even family camp outs for families with children ages four to fourteen! Make sure you check the website to see what's on offer!

Joppa Flats Education Center

1 Plum Island Turnpike, Newburyport

978-462-9998 | www.massaudubon.org; Search Joppa Flats

Also part of Mass Audubon, The Joppa Flats Education Center is located at the gateway to one of the country's most productive, year-round, wildlife viewing areas—the Parker River National Wildlife Refuge and the Plum Island estuary. Joppa Flats has a variety of programming for children—both preschool and school age. Some classes included Parent/Child Walkabouts and a hands-on science course called Imagine, Sing, and Learn—designed for the curious and active preschooler! Visit the website to find out about current offerings.

Merrimack Valley

Boston Sports Club
307 Lowell Street, Andover
978-475-3333 | www.mysportsclubs.com
Monday–Fridays, 5AM–9PM; Saturday–Sunday, 7AM–6PM.
Membership prices vary from $49 to $89 per month;
see website for details.

A The Boston Sports Club offers recreational athletic programs for kids from six months to fifteen years. The gym also has babysitting for children from three months to ten years.

Cedardale Health & Fitness
931 Boston Road, Haverhill
978-373-1596 | www.cedardale-health.net
Monday–Thursday, 5AM–11PM; Fridays, 5AM–9PM;
Saturday-Sunday, 5:30AM–9PM.

A Cedardale is a cutting-edge, multipurpose health and recreation center, complete with tennis courts, a pool, an indoor track, and even a spa. There's great child care, plus a ton of programming for kids and adults. Across the street, the Cedarland Family Fun Center has an indoor playspace with mini golf and a batting cage. Some families opt to buy a membership just for the summer for access to the pool. The club also offers a free three-day trial membership.

Maternal Health & Fitness
7 Hodges Street, North Andover
978-738-8080 | www.maternalhealthandfitness.com
An eight-week session is $99; $20 for drop-in classes.

Maternal Health & Fitness has an eight-week postpartum fitness class to get back in shape after the birth of your baby. Contact the instructor, Jen, at 781-858-6156 for information on class times and sessions.

Yang's Fitness Center

5 Dundee Park Drive, Andover
978-475-2020 | www.yangsfitnesscenter.com
See website for hours of operation.

A Yang's is a fitness center, martial arts studio, and yoga studio rolled into one. Try their seven-day free trial pass. Morning child care hours are available every day but Sunday.

◆4 Best Spots to Dine Out with Kids

Family-friendly restaurants on the North Shore

WHEN WE HAD our first baby, a friend gave us this sound advice: "If you want to go out to eat with the baby, find the rowdiest, noisiest place you can—no one will even notice if the baby cries." It seemed counter-intuitive at the time. Take our baby to a noisy, rowdy restaurant? But the moment she let loose a wild yawp, we knew this was one wise woman.

Back in the day when our first was still in her infant car seat, we managed to sneak in a few quiet dinners at some of our favorite haunts from our kid-free days. But we've got a bigger brood now. If your kids are like mine, they may not be able to sit still for long or use their "inside voices" consistently. We've had to change the way we dine out. Now, we look for more budget-friendly options with kid-friendly menu items. Or better yet, a place where the kids have some sort of activity to keep them entertained at the table so the adults can actually enjoy the exercise of going out to eat in the first place. (Think: Bertucci's for the play dough, or Fuddruckers for the arcade games, or Joe's Landing, where kids can watch the airplanes take off and land.) Some of the following restaurants are chains that cater to families, and others are unique North Shore finds.

Moms in the area recommend the following restaurants on the North Shore for their gluten-free menu options for kids:

- P.F. Chang's at the Northshore Mall in Peabody
- Woodman's in Essex
- Fortune Palace in Essex
- Outback Steakhouse in Peabody

North Shore Dining Family Style!

Cape Ann

Lobsta Land

84 Causeway Street, Route 128, Exit 12, Gloucester
978-281-0415 | www.lobstalandrestaurant.com
April–mid-December, Sunday–Thursday, 7AM–9PM;
Friday–Saturday, 7AM–9:30PM.

Don't let the location right off the highway scare you. You can't beat Lobsta Land for the food and the beautiful view of the marshes. It's a family-friendly, budget-friendly restaurant serving breakfast, lunch, and dinner daily. There are food options to suit even the most finicky eaters, plus delectable dishes for adult palates.

Lobster Pool Restaurant

329 Granite Street, Rockport
978-546-7808 | www.lobsterpoolrestaurant.com
April–December 13, 11:30AM–8:30PM.

The Lobster Pool is self-service, casual dining at its best. It is the place to go after a day spent at one of Cape Ann's beautiful beaches. Picnic tables overlook Ipswich Bay, and it's perfectly situated to view spectacular sunsets. There's a grassy area for kids to roam free while adults enjoy the ocean views. Lobster and other seafood is the specialty, but you'll also find hot dogs and hamburgers and other casual food on the menu. Cash and personal checks only.

Sugar Magnolias

112 Main Street, Gloucester
978-281-5310 | www.sugarmags.com
Tuesday–Saturday, 7AM–2:30PM;
Sundays, Sugar Mags serves breakfast only.

Winner of *Boston Magazine's* 2008 Best Breakfast award, Sugar Mags is a great place to take the family for breakfast or lunch. Get there early as there's often a line out the door. The food is definitely worth the wait.

Top Dog

2 Doyle Cove Road, Rockport
978-546-0006 | www.topdogrockport.com
Check website for hours of operation, which vary by season.

Kids will love this fun little hot dog shop that serves grilled and steamed hot dogs with unlimited toppings. It is a fairly tight space without table service, but kids can entertain themselves by drawing on the chalkboard walls. Afterwards, take the family for a stroll down Bearskin Neck for ice cream.

Woodman's

121 Main Street, Essex
800-649-1773 | www.woodmans.com

Zagat restaurant guide calls Woodman's an American cult classic right up there with baseball and apple pie. Famous for its fried clams, Woodman's is one restaurant where you won't need to worry about getting messy. The informal setting is perfect for families, but expect long lines in the summer. The menu includes clams, lobster, shrimp, scallops, chowder, and more—most of the seafood is fried. There are also hot dogs and burgers for non-seafood eaters, and there's a gluten-free menu.

Also try:

- Beach Street Café, Manchester-by-the-Sea
- Causeway Restaurant, Gloucester
- The Farm, Essex
- JT Farnham's, Essex
- Latitude 43, Gloucester

Greater Newburyport

Agawam Diner
Route 1, Rowley
978-948-7780

Open for breakfast and brunch, Agawam Diner is known for its great service, warm atmosphere, and traditional diner comfort foods. It's a family-friendly, budget-friendly option in Greater Newburyport, but note that it is cash only.

Black Cow
54 Merrimac Street, #R, Newburyport
978-499-8811 | www.blackcowrestaurants.com
Sunday–Thursday, 11:30AM–10PM; Friday–Saturday, 11:30AM–11PM.

The Black Cow in Newburyport is a touch upscale, but it's also a place where adults and kids alike can enjoy a great meal, a drink, and a beautiful atmosphere overlooking the water. It's worth the trip!

Cathy's Country Kitchen
300 Newburyport Turnpike, Rowley
978-948-3456
Tuesday–Thursday, 6AM–2PM; Saturdays, 6AM–1:30PM; Sundays, 7AM–

12:30PM (breakfast only on the weekends).

Cathy's Country Kitchen is a great place to bring the kids for breakfast and lunch. Everything is homemade. Patrons rave about the French toast, pancakes, breads and scones, and the service. Note that credit cards are not accepted, so come with cash in hand.

Flatbread Company

5 Market Square, Amesbury
978-834-9800 | www.flatbreadcompany.com
Sunday–Thursday, 11:30AM-9PM; Friday-Saturday, 11:30AM-9:30PM.

Flatbread is a popular spot for families, especially after sporting events when teams flock there for their popular brick oven pizza. There's often a line out the door, but many families choose to get takeout and sit outside.

Krueger Flatbread

142 Essex Street, Haverhill
978-372-3434 | www.kruegerflatbread.com
Monday–Thursday, 11:30AM-9:30PM; Friday-Saturday, 11:30AM-10:00PM; Sundays, noon-9PM.

Krueger serves all kinds of brick oven pizza, amazing salads, calzones, and sandwiches. Everything is cooked out in the open, and the pizza dough flipping through the air will keep the wee ones enthralled. Kids will be equally entertained at their tables, with pizza dough to play with and a supply of crayons and coloring books.

☙ Tea Party!

If you have a little one who loves tea parties, try a special one-on-one date at the Wenham Tea House. There's a monthly Children's Tea one Wednesday a month at 3:30PM, featuring an interactive story, games, songs, and crafts to take home. The cost is $20 per person, which includes refreshments for the children as well as a separate tea menu for the adults.

See www.wenhamteahouse.com for more details.

Village Pancake House

26 Main Street, Rowley
978-948-2211 | www.villagepancakehouse.com
Daily, 7:30AM–3PM; closed Thanksgiving and Christmas.

Breakfast served all day? Pancakes for lunch? Enough said! It's no wonder that the Village Pancake House is always hopping with young families. The restaurant is cash-only, but there is an ATM on the premises.

Also try:

- Abraham's Bagels, Newburyport
- Capaccio Italian Cuisine, Amesbury
- Oregano Pizzeria & Ristorante, Newburyport
- Stella's of Middle Street, Newburyport

Greater Salem

Bertucci's

27 Enon Street, Beverly
978-927-6866 | www.bertuccis.com
Daily, 11AM–10PM.

Yes, it's a chain restaurant, but Bertucci's is a big hit with the families, and the kids don't even mind the wait as long as they have their own personal pizza dough to play with at the table. The brick oven pizza and pasta dishes are delicious and affordable.

Border Café

356 Broadway, Saugus
781-233-5308 | www.bordercafe.com
Sunday–Thursday, 11:30AM–11PM; Friday–Saturday, 11:30AM–midnight.

The Border Café on Route 1 in Saugus is a crowd pleaser for families. They have a great special where kids get a drink, a meal, a dessert, and a balloon—all for $3.98! Adults will love the margaritas and Mexican food. Take the entire family out for dinner for the same price as going out to breakfast!

Engine House
71 Lafayette Street, Salem
978-745-1744 | www.enginehouserestaurant.com
Daily, 11AM–midnight.

The Engine House is known for its pizza, subs, and beer. They have a great kids' menu, and kids eat free on Tuesday nights from 5PM to 8PM, which makes it a popular place for parents in the Salem area. Some rules do apply: Kids under twelve must choose from the Fire Chief Jr. Menu, which has several options and includes a drink. Each child must be accompanied by an adult who is dining from the regular menu and spends at least $8.99.

O'Neill's Irish Pub
120 Washington Street, Salem
978-740-8811 | www.oneillsofsalem.com

Pubs and families do not normally a good mix make. But, countless families around the North Shore love to go to O'Neill's on Sunday afternoons for what has become an informal family day. There's a warm, inviting atmosphere complete with a roaring fire and a comfy leather couch. You'll see plenty of parents enjoying a beer while the kids dance to the live music and the entire crowd joins in on a rendition of "The Unicorn Song."

Family Fun Fridays in Marblehead

The Gerry No. 5 VFA in Marblehead hosts a Fabulous Family Friday that Marblehead parents love. Once a month on Fridays in the winter, the community gets together for a family-friendly meal including items like chicken fingers, hot dogs, fish, seafood, and pitchers of beer. The entire family can dine for less than $10, and the kids have plenty of room to play in the large function room.

Red's Sandwich Shop

15 Central Street, Salem
978-745-3527 | redssandwichshop.com
Monday–Saturday, 5AM–3PM; Sundays, 6AM–1PM.

Red's has won countless awards for its food, its atmosphere, and its service. It's a great place to take the kids for breakfast or lunch, as the food is delicious and comes quickly!

Something Different Café at Beverly Airport

3 LP Henderson Road, Beverly
978-927-0070 | www.beverlyairport.com

The Beverly Airport is a fun place to go for breakfast with kids. The restaurant is filled with airplane nostalgia, and you can sit and watch the planes and helicopters take off. The service can be slow, so go when you're not in a hurry (or when there is a lot of air traffic expected!).

Tokyo Japanese Steakhouse

300 Andover Street, #9, Peabody
978-532-8788

Tokyo Japanese Steakhouse is a great place for families, especially on Sundays, when kids eat free. (One free meal from the children's menu with the purchase of every adult meal.) The kids are kept well-entertained by the Japanese chefs who cook hibachi-style meals right at your table.

Also try:

- Acapulcos, Beverly
- The Barnacle, Marblehead
- Braccia's Four 66 Pub and Grille, Danvers
- Depot Diner, Beverly
- Driftwood Restaurant, Marblehead
- P.F. Chang's China Bistro at the Northshore Mall

Robin Abrahams is the weekly "Miss Conduct" columnist for *The Boston Globe Magazine* and author of the book *Miss Conduct's Mind over Manners*. Here's her advice:

- If table manners aren't important at home, they won't be important at a restaurant. Rehearse and reinforce the skills at home before opening night at Upstairs on the Square.

- Honor your children's biological needs. You can't expect a child to behave well if she's up two hours past her bedtime or is eating dinner at seven o'clock when her last snack was at two o'clock in the afternoon. Be aware, too, that kids are usually skeptical about new foods (this is universal and has evolutionary reasons). Expecting a child to eat escargot at nine in the evening is a recipe for disaster.

- If he has a meltdown, be prepared to take your kid out of the restaurant, and get him some other food pronto. This is consistent discipline for your child and shows courtesy to other patrons. It's always good to have a plan B in mind when taking your child out.

- Never, ever change a baby's diaper in a restaurant booth. (You wouldn't think I'd have to say that, but I've gotten letters about this!) Breastfeeding mothers complain that they shouldn't have to feed their babies in the bathroom, and they have a point. No one should have to eat in the bathroom—so don't turn your dining room into one.

- Sell your kids on the idea of table manners—and all manners—by presenting them as a way to be cool and grown-up.

Merrimack Valley

Andolini's

19 Essex Street, Andover
978-475-4811 | www.andolinisrestaurant.com
Sunday-Monday, 5PM-9PM; Tuesday-Saturday, 5PM-10PM.

Fans of Glory Restaurant are probably going to love its new iteration,

Andolini's, which features nostalgic Italian fare that it sure to make the whole family happy. Andolini's loves kids and aims to be the most kid-friendly restaurant in the area. Although the kid's menu is a touch limited (essentially, pasta and chicken fingers), the "make your own sundae," which is included, is sure to make up for it. There is also a beautiful patio for al fresco family fun!

 Clam Fest!

Memorial Park, Essex

Here's a great way to introduce the shortest members of your family to a New England culinary tradition: clam chowder. The Essex Clam-Fest, held in Memorial Park in Essex every fall, is a fun outing for the whole family. Local restaurants compete for the coveted People's Choice Award for best chowder. A $5 entry fee buys you a plastic spoon, all the chowder you can taste, and a ballot to place your vote. Non-chowder eaters will also find plenty of hot dogs, hamburgers, and lemonade stands, plus live music, goods from local artisans, and children's games (often even a pony ride). There's a playground on the premises for young kids, as well as clean bathroom facilities. You'll want to ditch the stroller and put the baby in a backpack or a carrier, as this event can draw a hungry crowd.

Fuddruckers
Locations in Saugus, North Andover, Reading
www.fuddruckers.com

Yup, another chain—but Fuddruckers is a great family-friendly and budget-friendly option that the whole family will enjoy. The Fuddruckers at Jordan's Furniture store in Reading is a particular hit with families, as kids love the ice cream shop, trapeze show/lessons, the taxi and fire engine shopping carts, and the fountain show. Some Fuddruckers also have arcade games. Since you'll need to carry your own tray of food to your table, you may want to go with a second pair of adult hands.

Joe's Landing Café

492 Sutton Street, North Andover, at the
Lawrence Municipal Airport
978-682-8822 | www.lawrencemunicipalairport.com
Open for breakfast and lunch daily.

North Shore families love to flock here for breakfast. Little aviators are so mesmerized by the airplanes that the adults can actually eat their breakfast in peace! Grab a table by the windows and try the banana and M&Ms pancakes for the kids.

The Loft

1140 Osgood Street, North Andover
978-686-0026
www.loftsteakandchophouse.com
Daily; see website for times, which vary.

Located in a one-hundred-sixty-year-old wooden barn, The Loft offers a classic New England feeling that's budget and family friendly. There's a good kids' menu, plus a full menu for adults, with a hearty emphasis on comfort foods—yum! Try the famous lobster mac and cheese.

☼ What's Cookin'?

Eurostoves, on Route 1A in Beverly, has some great hands-on cooking classes for parents and their children, taught by professional chefs. In the Cooking Fun with Mom or Dad classes, kids spend the afternoon cooking with a parent and get to bring home the dinner they've prepared. The classes last three hours and cost $79 per pair. ($40 for each additional person.) For ages three through six, there's a Backyardigans class ($49) where the kids learn to make things like quesadillas, turkey pouches, and apple triangles. There are also gingerbread house and cupcake classes, plus a Dora the Explorer cooking class ($49) where kids make some of Dora's favorite treats, like Backpack's Take Along Trail Mix, Benny's Fresh Blueberry Muffins, Boots' Bananarama Ding Dongs, Map's Rolled Up Soft Tacos, and Dora's Favorite Cupcake Cones.

See www.eurostoves.com for details.

Not Your Average Joe's

90 Pleasant Valley Street, Methuen
978-974-0015 | www.notyouraveragejoes.com
Monday–Thursday, 11:30AM–10PM; Friday–Saturday, 11:30AM–11PM;
Sundays, noon–10PM.

If your kids are old enough for a movie, head to Not Your Average Joe's in Methuen for dinner, and get discount movie tickets for AMC and Lowes theaters. There are families who go just for the bread and olive oil, but you'll also love the menu's wide selection of seafood, chicken, and pasta dishes.

Also try:

- Café Azteca, Lawrence
- Deleo's Pizza, Groveland
- Maria's Family Restaurant, Haverhill
- Palmer's Restaurant and Tavern, Andover
- Wichit, Lawrence

No Time to Cook?

These gourmet stores on the North Shore have some delicious—and healthy—options for takeout dinners that taste just like mom made them. (It'll be our little secret.)

- Bliss Gourmet Takeout, Beverly Farms
- Essen, Manchester-by-the-Sea
- Henry's Market, Beverly
- Shubie's Marketplace, Marblehead
- The Natural Grocer, Newburyport

5 Combating Cabin Fever
Fun rainy day and winter indoor activities

DURING CERTAIN TIMES of year, being a parent in New England requires some Yankee ingenuity. Recent winters have been so unkind to New England parents that shoveling out of the house is actually a welcome form of stress relief. If you can get out of the house and driveway, you'll be happy to know that there are plenty of playspaces, story times, museums, and activities at local libraries that will keep the four walls from closing in on you. And when there's not a blizzard on the horizon, get those kids outside. Remember: bears hibernate, not kids—and you and your little ones will survive the season intact if you make the most of the North Shore's winter wonderland!

Indoor Playspaces

YMCA of the North Shore
Locations in Cape Ann, Beverly, Haverhill, Ipswich, Salem, and Marblehead
978-922-0990 | www.northshoreymca.org
$88 per month for a two-adult family with children; some classes and programs have an additional fee.

A Seriously, where would my family be without the YMCA? We love it for their open gymnastics, open gym, family swim, the plethora of classes for kids, and the child care options that allow mom and dad to squeeze in a workout. The open gym, gymnastics, and pool times are free for members. Most facilities also have a snack shop. The North Shore YMCA also runs some very popular and affordable summer and vacation camps for kids. Worth noting is the Sterling Center in Beverly; this fabulous dance school, the Sterling School of Dance, holds classes for kids as young as three years old.

Cape Ann

Cape Ann Lanes
53 Gloucester Avenue, Gloucester
978-283-9753 | www.funbowling.com
See website for hours of operation.
Weekdays: $3.75 per string per person. Weekends, nights (after 5PM), holidays, and vacations: $4.25 per string per person. Bumper lane rental: $26 per hour or $13 per half hour. Shoe rental is $3 (socks are required).

P **E** Cape Ann Lanes is a fun place for the whole family on a cold or rainy day. The candle-pin style bowling is perfect for small kids, and bumpers are available for the littlest ones. There's a snack bar with pizza and other concession-type foods, and an arcade, so bring that piggy bank! Check out the Cape Ann Lanes birthday party packages as well.

☀ Happy Birthday!

Psssst ... **Hey, Mom: Why not let the kids smoosh their birthday cake frosting into someone else's carpet? In this section, you'll find some great ideas for hosting a hassle-free party. Most of the indoor playspaces around the North Shore offer party packages, where kids generally enjoy an hour of playtime and then have time for birthday cake and other treats. See the individual websites of the listings in this chapter for details.**

Greater Newburyport

123 Little Me
112 Parker Street, Newburyport
978-499-9123 | www.123littleme.com
See website for current hours of operation.
Open play is $10 and no reservations are required.

T **P** 123 Little Me is a popular year-round indoor playspace with climbing structures, hands-on edu-activities, and a craft area. Newburyport moms especially love the fact that you can drop off the kids for as long as three hours. Many moms will leave the kids to play while they get their shopping done.

Joe's Playland

15 Broadway and 12 Broadway, Salisbury
978-465-8311 | www.joesplayland.com

P **E** Joe's Playland is a family-run arcade in the center of Salisbury, featuring pinball, skeeball, prizes, a snack bar, and more. It's open year-round, but hours of operation vary by season, so check the website before you go.

Leo's Superbowl, Inc.

84 Haverhill Road, Amesbury
978-388-2010 | www.leossuperbowl.com
Monday–Thursday, 9AM–10PM; Fridays, 9AM–11PM;
Saturdays, 10:30–11PM; Sundays, 10:30AM–9PM.
Weekdays: $3.75 per person per game. Weekends, nights (after 5PM), and holidays: $4 per person per game. Bumper bowling: $24 per hour per lane, prorated by the minute. Shoe rentals are $1.75.

P **E** Kids will love to bowl, have a slice of pizza, and hit the arcade for some post-bowl games. Sal's/Mary's kitchen is available for food, and the bowling alley serves wine and beer for adults. Leo's has cosmic bowling on Friday evenings, featuring a glow-in-the-dark, dance-club atmosphere. Leo's also hosts birthday parties for kids.

Greater Salem

Bonkers Funhouse

535 Lowell Street, Peabody
978-535-8355 | www.bonkersfunhouse.com
Unlimited all day Rides & Maze pass is $15 per child; Monday–Wednesday Rides & Maze pass is $12 per child; Kiddie City for toddlers under three is free.

T **P** **E** Bonkers Funhouse is a pizza place "where family fun and great food come together." Check out Kiddie City while you're there—a free, toddler-only area. For the older kids, there's a Ferris wheel, a carousel, a huge Little Tykes maze, skeeball, air hockey, and more. The restaurant serves pizza, pasta dishes, and chicken wings. Take-out is available and socks are required.

Build-A-Bear Workshop at the North Shore Mall

210 Andover Street, Peabody
978-532-6588 | www.buildabear.com
Stuffed animals range in price from $10 to $25.

T **P** **E** At Build-A-Bear Workshops, kids can make their own stuffed animals using the provided supplies. Kids are able to choose from over thirty teddy bears, bunnies, dogs, and other stuffed animals. Once stuffed, the children take their bears (or animal of choice) to various stations to give the stuffed animal a unique personality by choosing from the outfits, accessories, embroidery options, sounds, and recordings. Birthday party packages start at $10 per guest.

CoCo Key Water Resort, Danvers

50 Ferncroft Road, Danvers
978-777-2500 | www.cocokeywaterresort.com
Check website for hours of operation.
Day passes are available based on water park capacity with certain restrictions and blackout dates; day passes should be reserved online to guarantee admission and are nonrefundable. Monday–Thursday day pass is $32 per person; Friday–Sunday day pass is $40 per person.

A Billed as New England's largest indoor water resort, CoCo Key features water slides, body flumes, a lazy river, a dip-in theater, a hot tub, and an arcade. Food is available from A&W, Pizza Hut, and the Wet Rooster Bar. Hotel rooms are also available for reservation if you want to make a weekend of it.

Mall Tots

Liberty Tree Mall, 100 Independence Way, Danvers
978-777-6411 | www.malltots.com
Monday–Saturday, 9AM–8PM; Sundays, 10AM–6PM.
$8 for the first child, $3 for each additional child; half price after 4PM every weekday. Buy a Fastpass to get ten visits for $60.

I T P Moms who are out running errands at the Liberty Tree Mall love to stop in at Mall Tots, which is adjacent to Kohl's department store. Toddlers through five-year-olds can run, play, and crawl on the slides and climbing structures. The ten-thousand-square-foot indoor playspace also includes bounce houses, tunnels, kick balls, soccer balls, and baseball equipment. The space is open for public play dates, and no reservations are needed. Parents are required to stay with children and are encouraged to play with children in the space. The per-child entry fee gives kids all-day access. Worth a note: Hip Baby Gear has a clearance section here, where you can find some good bargains. Birthday party packages are also available.

Marblehead Community Center

10 Humphrey Street, Marblehead
781-631-3350
$1 per child.

A On Mondays and Fridays, for a nominal fee, families can enjoy an open gym for small children. It's a great place to socialize with other moms and kids. Tip from the local moms: finish your latte in the car, as you can't bring your morning coffee inside!

Monkey Joe's

10 Newbury Street, Danvers Crossing Mall, Danvers
978-739-8099 | www.monkeyjoes.com
Monday–Saturday, 10AM–6PM; Sundays, 11AM–6PM.
Walk-in play is $9.99 per child, ages three and up;
children two and under are $5.

T P E Monkey Joe's is like kid heaven, with their plethora of giant inflatable bounce structures. It can be difficult keeping track of kids in the playspace when it's crowded, but there is a nice toddler area that's small and contained for the littlest tykes. Don't forget socks and your hand sanitizer. Concession foods and a snack area are available and outside food is not allowed. Monkey Joe's also has birthday party packages. Note that parents are required to be with kids at all times while they're at Monkey Joe's.

Monster Mini Golf

10 Newbury Street, Danvers
978-762-4800 | www.monsterminigolf.com
Year-round, Monday–Thursday, 10AM–9PM;
Fridays, 10AM–10PM; Sundays, 10AM–8PM.
Free admission to the facility; $6.50–$7.50 per person for eighteen holes.

P **E** Monster Mini Golf is an indoor monster-themed glow-in-the-dark eighteen-hole miniature golf course. There are arcade games and private party rooms for birthdays. The entire place (except the bathrooms) glows in the dark! While the monsters themselves are not *super* scary, some moms have noted that this adventure can be a bit frightening for the smaller kids.

Pump It Up

5B Webster Street, Peabody
978-532-JUMP | www.pumpitupparty.com
Pop-In Playtimes are $8 per child.

T **P** **E** Looking for a great way to get the kids to expend some energy on a rainy day? Try Pump It Up's Pop-In Playtimes on Tuesday and Wednesday mornings from 9:30AM to 11AM. For $8, kids can bounce, climb, slide, and jump in bouncy houses and other inflatable toys. No reservations are required, but socks are. Parents must accompany children.

Roller Palace and Soccer Etc.

130 Sohier Road, Beverly
978-927-4242 | www.rollerpalace.net
See website for current open skate schedules.
$7 per person includes skate rentals.

P **E** Local moms will tell you that this place hasn't changed much since the '70s. The carpet might be the same, but it's still a great place for kids' birthday parties, and for moms to take a roll down memory lane. There's also a year-round indoor soccer facility that's cool in the summer and warm in the winter, available for birthday parties and soccer leagues.

Strike One
199 Newbury Street (Route 1 North), Danvers
978-739-4700 | www.strikeone.com
Rookie program is $100 per player for a month-long session.

P **E** Strike One is an indoor baseball and sports facility with a rookie baseball program for kids as young as age five, which teaches basic hitting and throwing techniques, base running, and ground ball and fly ball fielding techniques. Birthday party packages are also available and should be booked way ahead of time as space is limited.

Merrimack Valley

aMAZEment Action Playcenter
931 Boston Road, Haverhill
978-521-7700 | www.cedarland.net
Monday-Saturday, 10AM-8PM; Sundays, 11AM-7PM
General admission is $7.95 for two to twelve years old; $4.95 for twelve to twenty-three months; free for twelve months and under.

A Part of the larger Cedarland facility, aMAZEment features a family-friendly Sports Court, a triple wave slide, a moon bounce, a special area for toddlers featuring a pretend store and house, a sand room, a chalk table, a train table, a tree house, a tot-sized bouncer, and a pedal-go-round. (Phew! The mere thought is exhausting!) There are also five private party rooms, and concession foods are available—after all this, your kids are sure to be hungry!

Imajine That

354 Merrimack Street, Lawrence
978-682-5338 | www.imajinethat.com
Monday–Thursday, 9AM–5PM; Friday–Saturday, 9AM–8PM;
Sundays, 9AM–5PM.
$8.95 for children one and up; $2.95 for babies under one; adults are $1.

T P E With its bouncy houses, slides, play structures, and learning centers, this indoor playspace is great for the two-through-seven age group. Other popular features include an enormous child-sized grocery store, a dinosaur climbing structure, a Between the Lions reading area, a pirate station, and arts and science stations. It's also of note that Imajine That and nearby Sal's Restaurant have partnered to offer a date night for parents: drop your children off at Imajine That for two hours of playtime and dinner while you enjoy a date at Sal's Restaurant. Now that's something worth writing about!

Jump On In

40 Rogers Road, Haverhill
978-372-3220 | www.jumponinfun.com
Wednesdays, 3:30PM-5:30PM;
Fridays, 10:30AM–12:30PM (open-gym hours).
$10 per child; $8 for additional siblings.

A One of the first inflatable playspaces in the area, Jump On In features inflatable bouncy houses, obstacle courses, slides, tunnels, mazes, and a trampoline basketball game that they promise is unlike anything you've ever seen. Open-gym hours are on Wednesdays and Fridays. (Parents must stay with the child for open-gym time.)

Little Monkey's Jungle Gym

439 South Union Street, Lawrence
978-975-3031

I T P Geared toward infants up to children age four, this is a great place to let the kids run around and wear themselves out! Kids will love the jumpy castle, train table, ride-on toys, art station, playhouse, and more.

Independent Toy Stores

Cape Ann

Crackerjacks

27 Whistlestop Mall, Rockport
978-546-1616
Monday–Saturday, 9AM–5PM.

Crackerjacks is one of the few places to buy toys for kids in Rockport. It's a great place to stock up on beach toys and other outdoor toys for kids. You'll also find plenty of seasonal and holiday decorations, toys, and arts and crafts supplies.

Happy Whale Toys

59 Bearskin Neck, Rockport
978-546-6311

This is a fun little shop with beach toys, stuffed animals, puppets, puzzles, games, and other toys.

Silly Goose

166 Main Street, Essex
978-768-4545 | www.usillygoose.com
Tuesday–Saturday, 10AM–6PM; Sundays, 11AM–6PM.

Silly Goose is a sweet little toy shop in downtown Essex that prides itself on offering fine American and European manufactured products that are not usually found in the big box stores. You can find plenty of classic and retro toys, outdoor toys, educational toys, and more.

Toodeloos

137 Main Street, Gloucester
978-281-2011 | www.toodleoos.com
Monday-Tuesday, 10AM-6PM; Friday-Saturday, 10AM-8PM;
Sundays, noon-5PM.

This happy little toy shop was designed to be the antithesis of the big box toy shops in the mall, and it's chock-a-block with wonderful gems for the younger set. What's more, there is a strong connection to the community at Toodeloos, and the owners have sponsored Police Safety Days (kids can sit in the cruiser!) and Firefighter Days (kids can climb into the engine!). Buy a toy at Toodeloos, and you'll feel good about shopping local.

Zak's

2 Beach Street, Manchester-by-the-Sea
978-526-1115 | www.zaksgifts.com
Monday–Friday, 10AM–5:30PM; Saturdays, 9:30AM–5PM;
Sundays, noon–5PM.

Zak's is a fun little boutique toy store with plenty of things for mom too. You'll find hand-crafted jewelry, soaps, candles, cards, hand-made chocolates, and tons of toys. It's a popular spot for Cape Ann moms who need to pick up a quick gift for a kid's birthday party.

Greater Newburyport

Eureka!

50 Water Street, Tannery Mill #1, Newburyport
978-465-9359 | www.eurekatoys.com
Monday–Saturday, 9AM–9PM; Sundays, 10AM–6PM.

Newburyport moms recommend Eureka! as the best place to buy fun, unique, educational, and budget-friendly birthday gifts—they're even wrapped for free. There's also a popular bookstore attached to the store.

Green Elephant Toys

3 Market Street, Ipswich
978-356-3636 | www.greenelephanttoys.com

Green Elephant Toys is a little toy shop carrying toys, games, puzzles, books and more, with brands including Playmobile, Lego, Schylling, Douglas, Folkmanis, Gund, and Mattel.

Greater Salem

The Learning Express
4 Enon Street, Beverly
978-927-1972 |
www.beverly.learningexpress-toys.com
Monday–Saturday, 9:30AM–5:30PM;
Sundays, noon–5PM.

32 Park Street, Andover
978-474-0555
www.andover.learningexpress-toys.com
Monday–Wednesday, 9:30AM–5:30PM;
Thursday–Friday, 9:30AM–8PM; Saturdays,
9:30AM–5PM; Sundays, 11AM–5PM.

A great place for innovative educational toys and games,
as well as the classics. You'll find great activities for kids with sensory
issues. Sign up for online coupons delivered to your inbox. The store
also holds classes for small kids that include stories and art projects.
See the website for details.

Marblehead Toy Shop
46 Atlantic Terrace, Marblehead
781-631-9900
Monday–Wednesday, Fridays, 9:30AM–5:30PM; Thursdays,
9:30AM–8PM; Saturdays, 9AM–5:30PM; Sundays, noon–5PM.

Marblehead Toy Shop is popular with local moms who
are running out to buy a last-minute birthday gift: you
can find some unique items and they gift wrap!

Mud Puddle Toys
1 Pleasant Street, Marblehead | 781-631-0814
221 Essex Street, Salem | 978-740-5400
www.mudpuddletoys.com
Monday–Saturday, 9:30AM–6PM; Sundays, 11AM–5:30PM.

Moms love Mud Puddle Toys for their unique toys, cool lunch boxes, Ugly Dolls, and the ability to find traditional toys like Legos, as well as organic and eco-friendly toys. Kids will love to play with the train tables set up in the back of the store while mom shops.

Greater Newburyport

Fiddlestix
25 Main Street, Amesbury
978-388-8070 | www.fiddlestix4fun.com
Tuesday–Thursday, 10:30AM–4PM; Fridays, 10:30AM–5PM; Saturdays, 10AM–4PM.

Fiddlestix carries books, dress-up clothes, games, and more from product lines such as Baby Einstein, Gund, Melissa & Doug, Lego, and Playmobil. They also have a free gift-wrapping service—perfect for when you're in a last-minute gift-giving pinch.

Bookstores with Story Times and Activities

Cape Ann

Manchester By the Book (Children's Room)
27 Union Street, Manchester-by-the-Sea
978-525-2929 | www.manchesterbythebook.com
Daily, 9AM–8PM.

Manchester By the Book has a small, but sweet, little children's room with plenty of children's books and some comfy bean bag chairs. The bookstore hosts ongoing children's events, such as fairy day, kids' craft day, kids' book clubs, and more. See the website for current events and information.

Toad Hall Bookstore

47 Main Street, Rockport
978-546-7323 | www.toadhallbooks.org
Monday–Saturday, 10AM–5PM; Sundays, 11AM–5PM.

While Toad Hall Bookstore doesn't offer much in the way of children's programming, it's worth mentioning for its fully-stocked kids room. Toad Hall has some great hand-selected titles, and the fact that the bookstore is a non-profit organization where all net proceeds go to environmental projects and education is fantastic.

Greater Newburyport

Bertram & Oliver Booksellers

5 Market Square, Amesbury
978-388-BOOK | www.bertramandoliver.com

This cozy little bookstore wants to instill a love of reading in all children. With occasional kids programs, and a true passion for the written word, you can't go wrong popping in to see what's on their shelves. Amesbury residents who have a newborn in tow can take advantage of Bertram & Oliver's Baby's First Book program, where you can choose your baby's first book—free!

The Book Rack

52 State Street, Newburyport
978-462-8615 | www.hugobookstores.com
Monday–Wednesday, 9AM–6PM; Thursday–Saturday, 9AM–8PM; Sundays, 11AM–5PM.

The Book Rack in downtown Newburyport has an amazing children's room, complete with colorful, fun kid-size chairs and Dr. Seuss wall hangings. The store hosts children's story time and yoga, plus plenty of other programming. See the website for current programming schedules and information.

Greater Salem

Banbury Cross Children's Bookshop
162 R Main Street (Route 1A), Wenham
978-468-4040 | www.banburybooks.com
Tuesday–Friday, 10AM–5PM; Saturdays, 10AM–4PM.

Banbury Cross is a beautiful little bookstore for small children. The staff are all children's literature specialists who use their extensive knowledge and expertise to help book buyers make appropriate selections. Banbury Cross also offers wonderful programming that introduces children to a love of reading early on. Classes are held throughout the North Shore. See Chapter 3 for more information.

Barnes & Noble Bookstores
Locations in Peabody and Saugus:

Northshore Mall
210 Andover Street, Peabody
978-573-3261 | www.barnesandnoble.com
Sundays, 10AM–9PM; Monday–Saturday, 9AM–10PM.
See website for children's story times and events.

The Thomas the Train table in the children's section gives small kids something to play with while you browse the books. Ask about their reading incentives programs, where kids can earn a free book by reading a certain number of books.

Staples Plaza
444A Broadway, Saugus
781-231-4711 | www.barnesandnoble.com
Sunday, 9AM–9PM; Monday–Saturday, 9AM–10PM.
See website for children's story times and events.

The Spirit of '76 Bookstore and Card Shop
107 Pleasant Street, Marblehead
781-631-7199 | hugobookstores.com
Monday–Friday, 8AM–8PM; Saturday, 8AM–6PM; Sunday, 11AM–5PM.

The Spirit of '76 has a great children's room, as well as a story hour and children's events. See the website calendar of events for current programming.

Merrimack Valley

Andover Bookstore
89 Main Street, Andover
978-475-0143 | www.hugobookstores.com
Monday–Friday, 8AM–8PM; Saturdays, 8AM–6PM; Sundays, 11AM–5PM.

The Andover Bookstore has a great children's section with story times. The bookstore has been around for two hundred years and is a cozy place to visit, with its fireplace, coffee, cookies, and comfy chairs.

Movies

Cape Ann

Gloucester Cinema
74 Essex Avenue (Route 133), Gloucester
978-283-9188 | www.gloucestercinema.com
Children twelve and under are $7; matinees before 6PM are $7.

P **E** Gloucester Cinema shows plenty of family-friendly movies, with low-cost matinees before 6PM. See website for current features and show times.

Greater Newburyport

Cinemagic
6 Merrill Street, Route 110, Salisbury
978-499-9494 | www.cinemagicmovies.com

P **E** At Cinemagic, you can stretch out in stadium seating and see all the latest IMAX 3-D movies.

Here are a few other bookstores in and around the North Shore that are definitely worth a visit:

Jabberwocky Bookshop

50 Water Street, Newburyport
978-465-9359 | www.jabberwockybookshop.com

Jabberwocky carries kids books and has a wonderful partnership with Eureka, the educational toy store next door, bringing children's books and toys together in a delightful way.

Bookshop of Beverly Farms

40 West Street, Beverly Farms
978-927-2122 | www.realbookshop.com

Founded in 1968, the Book Shop has been a thriving enterprise ever since, offering a great selection of fun toys, puzzles, books, and activities for young people of all ages—as well as great books for the grown ups in their lives. The Book Shop also is a great resource for local schools.

Derby Square Bookstore

215 Essex Street, Salem
978-745-8804

You'll definitely be able to find some great children's books in this shop, but you may not want to bring your toddler with you to hunt for them. If you're a bibliophile with a babysitter, hit this wonderful treasure trove of towering titles on your own! All books are said to be hand selected and fifty percent off.

Annie's Book Stop

132 Dodge Street, Beverly
978-922-0028 | www.anniesbooks.com

According to the owners, Annie's Book Stop has been the leading "pre-read" book stores since the early 1970's. Bargain hunters rejoice!

Well Read Books

37 Plaistow Road, Plaistow, NH
603-819-5116 | www.wellreadbookstore.com

Just over the border, in sales-tax-free New Hampshire, is the gem of a bookstore, Well Read Books. If that's not enough to lure you over state lines, then their comfy kid's corner may entice you.

Greater Salem

Cinema Salem

1 East India Square, Salem
978-744-1400 | www.cinemasalem.com; Search: Mom & Baby

A Cinema Salem has Mom & Baby shows every Monday at 10AM, where you can enjoy a first-run movie while still caring for your bundle of joy. The cinema keeps the lights brighter and sound quieter, and little ones are encouraged to yell and scream all they want. There's a changing table in the lobby, and mother's groups are encouraged to attend.

The Community House of Hamilton & Wenham Movie Programs

284 Bay Road, South Hamilton
978-468-4818 | www.communityhouse.org
See website for current schedule of events.
$3 includes movie, beverages, and munchies.

P **E** The Hamilton-Wenham Community House offers family-friendly outdoor movies in the summer and indoor movies in the winter. During the holidays, there's a very affordable babysitting program where you can drop the kids off for a movie, then head out for a few hours of kid-free shopping.

Hollywood Hits Movies for Moms

7 Hutchinson Drive, Danvers
978-777-4000 | www.hhdt.com; Click: Movies for Moms
See website for show times and listings.

I Hollywood Hits offers matinee movies for moms who want to come with infants or small children in tow. Babies are free, and the movies are geared toward moms. Lights are kept on dim so moms can see if they need to feed a baby or take care of a toddler, and sound is kept low—baby talk is welcome. Changing tables are available, and there's stroller access and storage available.

IMAX Theater at Jordan's Furniture

50 Walkers Brook Drive, Reading
781-944-9090 | www.jordans.com
Monday–Saturday, 10AM–10PM; Sundays, noon–6PM.
Ticket prices range from $6.50 to $11.50, with a $1.25 fee for 3-D glasses.

A The Jordan's Furniture store in Reading features some great family-friendly IMAX movies. Have lunch at Fuddruckers, catch a movie, and then take the kids for a post-movie ice cream cone. They'll love watching the fountain show and the trapeze displays. And hey—you might even be able to squeeze in a bit of furniture shopping.

☼ Date Night

Put the kids in bed and have a North Shore movie date night! Load your Netflix account with some of the following movies featuring the North Shore and try to spot places you know: *The Good Son*, *The Perfect Storm*, *The Witches of Eastwick*, *Stuck on You*, *The Proposal*, and *Grown Ups*.

Merrimack Valley

Chunky's Cinema Pub

371 Lowell Avenue, Haverhill
978-374-2200 | www.chunkys.com
Admission is $7.25; matinees are $5.75.

P **E** At Chunky's Cinema Pub, you'll be seated at a table in reclining leather limousine chairs. Waiters take your lunch or dinner orders while you enjoy pub-style food and a movie. See the website for show times and menu selections, and be sure to arrive early to buy tickets.

Libraries

All of the local town libraries offer free story times and other programs for children. While you're there, why not check out some new books or

DVDs for the kids. Check with these libraries for the most up-to-date hours and program information:

Cape Ann

Essex Town Library (TOHP Burnham Library)
30 Martin Street, Essex
978-768-7410 | www.essexma.org

The Essex Town Library offers weekly story hours for small children. See the website calendar of events for times and events.

Manchester-by-the-Sea Public Library
15 Union Street, Manchester
978-526-7711 | www.manchesterpl.org

The library offers laptime stories for infants through two years of age, with rhymes, instruments, and simple books. There's also a preschool story time for three to five year olds with stories and simple crafts. See the website for events and times.

Rockport Public Library
17 School Street, Rockport
978-546-6934 | www.rockportlibrary.org

The Rockport Public Library has many programs for small children, featuring stories, magic, animals, and other Go Green programs. See the website calendar of events for details.

Sawyer Free Library
2 Dale Avenue, Gloucester
978-281-9763 | www.sawyerfreelibrary.org
See website for hours and schedules, as they change often.

Preschool story times are Tuesday through Friday mornings during the school year. There are also special programs and events for children and families, featuring a wide variety of performing artists. The Parent/Child Book Group meets on the last Thursday of every month.

Greater Newburyport

Amesbury Public Library
149 Main Street, Amesbury
978-388-8148 | www.amesburylibrary.org

The Amesbury Public Library offers a Mother Goose on the Loose program for babies that incorporates music, movement, ritual, repetition, positive reinforcement, developmental tips, nursery rhymes, illustrations, puppets, musical instruments, colored scarves, and book reading into a fun-filled thirty-minute session for children with their parent or caregiver. Registration is not required, but space is limited, so the program is on a first-come, first-served basis. Preschool story times are also offered for two-year-olds and three- to five-year-olds. Registration is not required. See the website for upcoming times and events.

Ipswich Public Library
25 North Main Street, Ipswich
978-356-6648 | www.ipswichlibrary.org

Story time programs are held three times a week from October through May. The Tuesday half-hour story time for children thirty months to three years of age includes stories, songs, and concludes with circle games. Children must be accompanied by an adult. Wednesday and Thursday half-hour programs for children three to five years old cover theme stories with games, songs, and a related craft project. All story time programs are free of charge, but registration is required.

Merrimac Public Library
86 West Main Street, Merrimac
978-346-9441 | www.merrimaclibrary.org

The Merrimac Public Library offers creative movement, crafts, and story time programs for young children. See the website for upcoming events.

Newbury Town Library
0 Lunt Street, Byfield
978-465-0539 | www.newburylibrary.org

Story hours are offered for two- and three-year-olds, and also for four- and five-year-olds. Programs include stories, a large motor skill activity, and a theme related craft. See the website calendar for days and times.

Newburyport Public Library
94 State Street, Newburyport
978-465-4428 | www.newburyportpl.org

The Children's Room offers regular special programs and events throughout the year, including sing-alongs, storytellers, magicians, animal programs, special art and craft projects, and science programs. Story times are offered for children from eighteen months to six years old. All story times require advance registration. The Mother Goose story time is a half hour of songs, and short stories for children eighteen months to thirty-five months old with a parent or caregiver participating. The story time for three-year-olds includes a craft project, and the story time for children four to six years includes an independent craft project. See website for most updated days and times.

Rowley Free Public Library
141 Main Street, Rowley
978-948-2850 | www.rowleylibrary.org

The Rowley Public Library offers free story times, sing-along music programs, Go Green crafts, a Lego club, yoga, and more. See the calendar of events online for times and details.

West Newbury Library (GAR Memorial Library)
490 Main Street, West Newbury
978-363-1105 | www.westnewburylibrary.org

Story hours are held for children ages six months to six years, including Babies and Books for infants and toddlers, ages six months to two years; Toddler Time for children ages two to three; and story hours for kids ages three to six years. Programs include stories, songs, games, and simple crafts for older kids.

The North of Boston Library Exchange (NOBLE) is a cooperative effort of twenty-eight area libraries founded to improve library service through automation and shared resources, which means that if you have a library card for one of these libraries, you can tap into the books and information available at all of them. Seventeen public library members, ten academic libraries, and one special library are members of NOBLE.

Greater Salem

Abbot Public Library
235 Pleasant Street, Marblehead
781-631-1481 | www.abbotlibrary.org

The Abbot Public Library offers story, music, and arts and crafts programs for small children. See the website calendar for upcoming programs.

Beverly Public Library
32 Essex Street, Beverly
978-921-6062 | www.beverlypubliclibrary.org

Baby, toddler, and preschool programs are offered. See the website calendar of events for details and times.

Flint Public Library
1 South Main Street, Middleton
978-774-8132 | www.flintlibrary.org

The library offers story times, puppet shows, crafts, and more. See the website calendar of events for details.

Hamilton-Wenham Public Library
14 Union Street, South Hamilton
978-468-5577 | www.hwlibrary.org

The Hamilton-Wenham Library offers a weekly thirty-minute Baby Book-worms class for ages newborn to eighteen months that includes stories and songs. There's also a weekly hour-long story time for children aged eighteen to thirty months. Children must be accompanied by their caregiver, and alternate care for siblings is encouraged. In-person registration is required for both programs. Preschoolers and kindergartners will enjoy the Monday night Pajama Storytime, a forty-five-minute story program. See website for most updated days and times.

Haverhill Public Library
99 Main Street, Haverhill
978-373-1586 | www.haverhillpl.org

Story times, games, crafts, and other programs are offered for small children. See the website calendar of events for details on upcoming events.

Lynn Public Library
5 North Common Street, Lynn
781-595-0567 | www.noblenet.org/lynn

See the online calendar for upcoming children's programs and events.

Lynnfield Public Library
18 Summer Street, Lynnfield
781-334-5411 | www.noblenet.org/lynnfield

The Lynnfield Public Library has a free weekly story time for kids ages two to three years on Mondays at 10AM. The story time includes songs and crafts. On Wednesdays at 10AM, there's a Mother Goose story time program for infants and toddlers, up to twenty-four months. Drop-ins are welcome for both programs.

Nahant Public Library
15 Pleasant Street, Nahant
781-581-0306 | www.nahant.org

The Nahant Public Library offers a free story hour program called Read with Your Kids, for children ages two to five on Thursdays at 11AM. Parents can request certain stories by calling a week in advance.

Peabody Institute Library of Danvers
15 Sylvan Street, Danvers
978-774-0554 | www.danverslibrary.org

Children's programs include Story Times, Fun Times, performers, and craft sessions. See the library calendar for upcoming events.

Peabody Libraries

Main Branch
82 Main Street, Peabody
978-531-0100 | www.peabodylibrary.org

South Branch Library
78 Lynn Street, Peabody
978-531-3380 | www.peabodylibrary.org

West Branch Library
603 Lowell Street, Peabody
978-535-3354 | www.peabodylibrary.org

All branches offer story times for babies and preschoolers, plus crafts and pajama parties for bigger kids. See the website for the upcoming calendar of events.

Saugus Public Library
295 Central Street, Saugus
781-231-4168 | www.saugus.ma.us/Library

The Saugus Public Library offers a toddler story time for two-year-olds and a theme-based preschool story time for children ages three to five. See the website for upcoming dates and times.

Swampscott Public Library
61 Burrill Street, Swampscott
781-596-8867 | www.noblenet.org/swampscott

The Swampscott Public Library offers an array of programs for small children, including Messy Mondays crafts for children ages two to five; Colorful Crafts for ages four and up; American Girl programs for ages six and up; yoga for ages two to four; and even a paper airplane workshop for young aviators ages six and up. And that's just the tip of the iceberg in terms of offerings; see the website calendar of events for details.

Topsfield Town Library
1 South Common Street, Topsfield
978-887-1528 | www.topsfieldtownlibrary.org

The Topsfield Friends of the Library program is a great resource for frequent updates about events at the library and in the Topsfield community. Contact the library to sign up.

Merrimack Valley

Boxford Village Libraries

East Village Library
10 Elm Street, Boxford
978-887-7323 | www.boxfordlibrary.org

Weekly story times are offered for children ages three to five years old, featuring books, puppets, and crafts. See the website calendar of events for days and times.

West Village Library
Washington Street, Boxford
978-352-7323 | www.boxfordlibrary.org

Georgetown Peabody Library
2 Maple Street, Georgetown
978-352-5728 | www.georgetownpl.org

The Georgetown Peabody Library offers many story time, craft, music, and hands-on exploration classes for small children. See the website calendar for upcoming events.

Lawrence City Libraries

Main Branch
51 Lawrence Street, Lawrence
978-620-3600 | www.lawrencefreelibrary.org

South Lawrence Branch
135 Parker Street, Lawrence
978-620-3650 | www.lawrencefreelibrary.org

The Children's Room offers stories, crafts, magic shows, and music and movement for all ages. See the website calendar for upcoming events.

Nevins Memorial Library
305 Broadway, Methuen
978-686-4080 | www.nevinslibrary.org

The Babies and Books program is designed to promote early literacy through rhymes, songs, and stories. Babies and toddlers up to the age of two are welcome with their caregivers. Big sibs are welcome to join in. Registration is not required.

Stevens Memorial Library
345 Main Street, North Andover
978-688-9505 | www.stevensmemlib.org

The Stevens Memorial Library offers a preschool story hour and a kindergarten story time. To check for openings and to sign up for programs, call the Children's Room: 978-688-9538.

Museums

Cape Ann

Cape Ann Museum, Gloucester
27 Pleasant Street, Gloucester

978-283-0455 | www.capeannmuseum.org
Tuesday–Saturdays, 10AM–5PM; Sundays, 1PM–4PM.
Adults, $8; Cape Ann residents, seniors, and students, $6; children under twelve, free. During the month of January, admission is free to all Cape Ann residents.

A Learn about Cape Ann's history, culture, and community. The museum has exhibits on Fitz Henry Lane, the fishing industry, the granite industry, historic homes, plus other special exhibits.

Essex Shipbuilding Museum
66 Main Street, Essex
978-768-7541 | www.essexshipbuildingmuseum.org
Year-round; see website for hours, which change seasonally.
Adults, $7; children age six to eighteen, $5; children under six, free.

A If you have any little boat lovers on your hands, they'll love the Essex Shipbuilding Museum, where they can see and touch the tools used to build a schooner, see the rigged ship models, and stand before a real wooden schooner. Mom will love a stroll through the nearby antique shops.

Gloucester Maritime Heritage Center
23 Harbor Loop, Gloucester
978-281-0470 | www.gloucestermaritimecenter.org
May–October; see website for hours.
Adults, $6; seniors, $5; children, $3; family maximum, $12.

A Situated on Gloucester's working waterfront, the maritime heritage center gives kids a chance to get up close and personal with marine life. Indoor and outdoor exhibits teach kids about the fishing industry, boatbuilding, and marine science. There are also fishing history and marine railway exhibits, as well as an aquarium. Don't miss the touch tanks!

Hammond Castle Museum
80 Hesperus Avenue, Gloucester
978-283-7673 | www.hammondcastle.org
See website for hours of operation, which change seasonally.

Adults, $10; seniors, $8; children, $6.

A Kids will love a tour through this medieval-style castle, which focuses on both medieval life and the castle's unique collection of artifacts—not to mention a visit to the tower dungeon! (You better eat your lunch or else!) Parents will love the view overlooking Gloucester Harbor. In October, the castle hosts its annual Castle of the Damned Spooktacular ($15 per person ages fourteen and up; $12 per each child six to thirteen). This is a PG-13 show and is **not** recommended for younger children.

Greater Newburyport

Custom House Maritime Museum
25 Water Street, Newburyport
978-462-8681 | www.thechmm.org
May–December, Tuesday–Saturday, 10AM–4PM;
Sundays and holiday Mondays, noon–4PM.
Adults, $7; children under six, free.

E Learn about Newburyport's maritime history, with its collection of model clipper ships, maritime art and artifacts, displays of famous shipwrecks, and more.

Ipswich Museum
54 South Main Street, Ipswich
978-356-2811 | www.ipswichmuseum.org
May–October; see website for hours.
Adults, $10; children ages six to twelve, $3; children under six, free.

A Throughout the year, the Ipswich Museum hosts family events and summer workshops for children. They also have a new after-school archaeology program and podcasts of important museum lectures. In October, there's a Kids' Halloween Party, featuring a haunted house, scary stories, scarecrow building, crafts, snacks, and a costume parade ($5 per child and members; $6, non-members; family cap at $20 for members and $24 for non-members). See the calendar of events for additional family activities throughout the year.

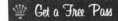
Many North Shore libraries offer free or discounted passes to museums in Greater Boston and around the North Shore. Passes are usually reserved on a first-come, first-served basis, so be sure to call well ahead of the date that you'd like to go.

Greater Salem

The Exchange at the Wenham Tea House
4 Monument Street, Wenham
978-468-1398 | www.wenhamteahouse.com
See website for hours of operation.

A Check out the world-renowned doll collection, model trains, and interactive exhibits of colonial times, including costumes, quilts, and toys. On Tuesday afternoons, the dining room can be rented for $100 to accommodate children's birthday parties, where you can choose from the daily tea menu—a great idea for a little girl's dress-up tea party.

The House of the Seven Gables
115 Derby Street, Salem
978-744-0991 | www.7gables.org
November–June, 10AM–5PM; July–October, 10AM–7PM.
Closed Thanksgiving, Christmas, and the first two weeks of January.
Adults, $12.50; children ages five to twelve, $7.50.

A Experience some of the country's earliest architecture in the house that Captain John Turner built in 1668. Visit the Kid's Cove for an interactive family experience. Climb up the famous secret staircase. Walk through the gardens and enjoy views of Salem Harbor, then stop in the café for lunch.

New England Pirate Museum
274 Derby Street, Salem
978-741-2800 | www.piratemuseum.com

May–October, daily, 10AM–5PM; weekends in April and November.
Adults, $8; children ages four to thirteen, $6.

A Perfect for budding pirates, who get to board a full-size recreation of a pirate ship and walk through an eighty-foot cave. You never know when you might spot a real pirate!

North Shore Children's Museum
294 Essex Street, YMCA Building, Salem
978-741-1811 | www.northshoreymca.org;
Search: Salem Family Room
Daily, 8:30AM–1:30PM.
North Shore YMCA members are admitted free;
check website for non-member fees.

T **P** **E** The North Shore Children's Museum, also known as the Salem YMCA Family Room, is a small but fun area where kids can play dress-up or post office, engage in creative play in a craft area, try hands-on learning experiments, drive a fire truck, and more. The center is also open for birthday parties, but space is limited.

Peabody Essex Museum
161 Essex Street, Salem
866-745-1876 | www.pem.org
Tuesday–Sunday and holiday Mondays, 10AM–5PM.
Adults, $15; children sixteen and under, free.

A Go for the day, visit the hands-on kids' exhibits, have lunch in the bright café, and look for treasures in the eclectic gift shop. Don't miss the two-hundred-year-old Chinese house (which costs extra) or the expansive children's area. On Saturdays and Sundays from 1PM to 3PM, museum educators lead hands-on arts projects for kids, inspired by the exhibitions (free with regular museum admission). The museum is very family-friendly, with strollers available on loan from the coat room, baby-changing stations in all restrooms, and secluded areas for nursing on most floors.

Salem Witch Museum

19 $^{1/2}$ Washington Square North, Salem
978-744-1692 | www.salemwitchmuseum.com
Daily, 10AM–5PM; July and August until 7PM.
Adults, $9.50; children ages six to fourteen, $6.50.

A Visit for Halloween, or year-round, to learn about the Salem Witch Trials of 1692 and the history of witches from pagan times to the present.

Wenham Museum

132 Main Street, Wenham
978-468-2377 | www.wenhammuseum.org
Tuesday–Sunday, 10AM–4PM; closed certain Mondays and holidays. See website for details.
Adults, $7.50; children ages one to eighteen, $5.50.

A Take the kids to learn how we lived, worked, dressed, and played in the seventeenth century. There's an international doll collection, toy soldiers, model trains, and old-fashioned wooden toys. The museum also offers drop-in craft classes as well as classes on Colonial times.

Witch Dungeon Museum

16 Lynde Street, Salem
978-741-3570 | www.witchdungeon.com
April–November, daily, 10AM–5PM.
Adults, $8; children ages four to thirteen, $6.

E Take a guided tour of the dungeon and Gallows Hill. Reenactments of witch trials may not be suitable for all ages.

Witch History Museum

197-201 Essex Street, Salem
978-741-7770 | www.witchhistorymuseum.com
April–November, daily, 10AM–5PM.
Adults, $8; children ages four to thirteen, $6.

E Historically accurate live presentations and fifteen life-size scenes depict the stories of the Salem Witch Trials, which may not be suitable for younger kids.

Merrimack Valley

The American Textile History Museum
491 Dutton Street, Lowell
978-441-0400 | www.athm.org
Wednesday–Sunday, 10AM–5PM.
Adults, $8; children ages six to sixteen, $6; museum members and kids under six, free.

E At the American Textile History Museum, kids get a chance to see how textiles impact their everyday lives. They can weave on an authentic hand-loom, try on a firefighter's flame-resistant coat, see clothing made from recycled plastic soda bottles, and more.

Outdoor Activities

There's so much beautiful open space on the North Shore of Boston that a long, snowy winter can present an endless array of options for kids to grab their sleds and hit the local park or a nearby hill for some free outdoor entertainment. Families can also find tons of options for snowshoeing and cross-country skiing on the area's many outdoor trails. (See the *A to Z List of Hiking and Biking Trails* on page 137.) Here are a few more ideas for getting out and enjoying all that a North Shore winter has to offer:

Ice Skating

Cape Ann

The Dorothy Talbot Rink
O'Maley Middle School, 32 Cherry
Street, Gloucester
978-281-9856
www.gloucesterschools.com
Public skating sessions are
November–mid-April,
Saturdays, 9AM.
*Learn to Skate program is $195
for twenty weeks.*

The Dorothy Talbot Rink is
home to the Gloucester High Fishermen Boy's Hockey program and the
Rockport Vikings. Starting in November through mid-April, the rink offers
several public skating sessions a week. (See the website for most updated
schedules.) Skate rentals are available, and the rink is also available on
an hourly basis for birthday parties and other events. The Learn to Skate
program, for ages three through eight, teaches kids about balance, stride,
edges, and stopping. Elbow and knee pads are recommended, and skates,
helmets, gloves/mittens are required.

Greater Newburyport

Graf Rink
28 Low Street, Newburyport
978-462-8112 | www.grafrink.com
See website for most updated schedules.
*Public skating admission is $5 for adults, $3 for kids and seniors.
Skate rentals, $5.*

The Graf Rink offers a range of year-round ice skating programs, such as
figure skating, ice hockey, learn-to-skate programs, and Tiny Tots. The

Tiny Tots classes are $120 for an eight-week session. Children must be at least three years old and have close to a fifty-minute attention span. For kids who have aged out of the Tiny Tots program, there's also a Basic Skills Learn to Skate program. Pre-registration is required for all classes, helmets must be worn, and equipment is available for rent.

Greater Salem

Connery Memorial Arena
182 Shepard Street, Lynn
781-599-9474 | www.fmcicesports.com
See website for most updated schedules and costs.

The Connery Memorial Arena offers public skating sessions and Learn to Skate programs, plus equipment rentals, birthday parties, a pro shop, and a snack bar.

Hockey Town USA, Inc.
953 Broadway, Saugus
781-233-3666 | www.hockeytownsaugus.com

Hockey Town USA offers a Mighty Duck Learn to Skate program for kids ages three to six. The five-week sessions are held on Monday afternoons and Tuesday mornings, for a $60 fee. The program is intended to provide an introduction to the skating and hockey environment. Skates and helmets are available for rent on a daily basis.

The James McVann-Louis O'Keefe Memorial Rink
511 Lowell Street, Peabody
978-535-2110 | www.peabodyskating.org
October–April.

This rink has public skating sessions along with adult and youth ice hockey. They also offer ice skating lessons to all skill levels and host birthday parties. Call for more information.

Pingree School Johnson Rink
537 Highland Street, South Hamilton
978-468-6232 | www.pingree.org
October–April.

The Pingree School's Learn to Skate program for tots ages three to six is held on Wednesday and Friday afternoons; there are also public skate sessions on weekend mornings. Call for the most up-to-date schedules and costs.

Rockett Arena Ice Skating Rink
225 Canal Street, Salem
978-542-6556 | www.salemstate.edu
October–April.

The Salem State Rockett Arena offers public ice skating sessions in the winter months. See the website for the most recent schedules and costs.

The Topsfield Fairgrounds
207 Boston Street, Topsfield
978-887-5000

This is a fun place to go skating if you live in the Topsfield area. You'll see tons of kids skating with crates on the iced-over parking lot. There's also a great hill for sledding across the street.

Ski School

Ski Bradford
60 South Cross Road, Bradford
978-373-0771 | www.skibradford.com

T P E Just outside of Haverhill, Ski Bradford offers lessons and ski school for kids as young as three years old. Moms say that the ski school is very well run and very well controlled. Four-week sessions run on weekend mornings and afternoons, for about $95. (Rental equipment for the four-week session is $45.) There's also a Little Rider snowboard program for $140 for ages six to seven. (Rental equipment for the four weeks is $55.)

Maple Sugaring at the Massachusetts Audubon Society

87 Perkins Row, Topsfield
978-887-9264 | www.massaudubon.org/ipswichriver
Tours are Saturdays and Sundays in March; see website for schedules.
Pre-registration required.
Adult member, $7.50; child member, $6.50. Adult non-member, $8.50; child non-member, $7.50. Children under three, free, and should be in a backpack.

Take the kids on an outdoor adventure to learn how to identify a sugar maple, observe tapping and sap collection methods, and watch the sap being boiled down in the sugar house, where everyone gets a sweet taste of the final product. Afterwards, warm up in the barn by the woodstove and try a hot dog cooked in maple sap. Syrup is available for sale. Tours last about an hour, rain or shine.

Maple Sugaring at the Breakheart Reservation

177 Forest Street, Saugus
781-233-0834 | www.saugus.org/FOBR
Seeking signs of spring? Look for the smoke rising from Breakheart's maple sugaring evaporators. Visit in March to learn how to identify maple trees in the winter, how to tap a tree, and how to boil sap. Enjoy pancakes and syrup around a campfire when your work is done. Call ahead for details and to register.

Turtle Lane Maple Farm
25 Turtle Lane, North Andover
978-258-2889 | www.turtlelanemaplefarm.com

Turtle Lane Maple Farm is a small, family-operated sugar house that uses a mix of old techniques and new technologies for maple sugaring. Tours are by appointment. Call or see website for the schedule.

Merrimack Valley

Brooks School Rink

1160 Great Pond Road, North Andover
978-686-6101 | www.nayouth.com/public-skating-at-brooks.html

The North Andover Figure Skating Club offers skating lessons at the Brooks School on Saturday mornings from November through March. Children must be four years old by September 1. Younger children with prior formal skating instruction may be accepted. The season includes approximately sixteen weeks of lessons for $240 per skater. Discounts are available to immediate family members, three or more skaters only. Helmets and mittens must be worn. In the past, the school has also held public skating sessions on Sunday evenings.

⚜ More Winter Fun

Don't forget to check out the Trustees of Reservations and Mass Audubon for their programs in the winter months. Many locations offer special classes throughout the season—it's a great way to get outside and stave off the winter doldrums!

Methuen High School
1 Ranger Road, Methuen
978-681-1345 | www.methuen.k12.ma.us; Search: Skating
Adults, $5; skating students, $3.

Methuen High School has public skating sessions on Saturday and Sunday afternoons from 1PM to 2PM, starting in mid-November. Helmets are required.

The Phillips Academy Ice Rinks
254 Main Street, Andover
978-684-7200 | www.andover.edu; Search: Ice Rink

The Phillips Academy Skating School offers group skating lessons throughout the year for all ages and abilities, including tots lessons. The hockey school also offers private lessons for anyone who wants individualized attention.

Valley Forum Ice Arena
654 South Union Street, Lawrence

7 Parkridge Road, Haverhill
978-557-5521/5518 | www.valleyrinks.com
Two-hour public skate: Adults, $12; twelve and under, $9.
One-hour public skate: Adults, $9; twelve and under, $7.

The Lawrence and Haverhill Valley Forum has public skating sessions every weekday from 11AM to 1PM. Skate rentals are not available. There is no public skating during school vacations and holidays. Learn to Skate programs are also held in both locations.

Veterans Memorial Ice Rink
229 Brook Street, Haverhill
978-373-9351 | ci.haverhill.ma.us; Search: Skating
Adults, $3; children under twelve, $1. Skate rental, $5.

Veterans Memorial has a Learn to Skate session on Sunday mornings starting in November and Tiny Tots classes for kids six and under on Tuesday mornings ($50 for a six-week session). See the website for current schedules.

6 Hot Stuff
Summer fun!

THERE'S NO BETTER time than summer to enjoy the great outdoors on the North Shore. From about April through October, you'll notice that people around the North Shore are suddenly very, very happy. Why shouldn't they be? Being here during those months is like being on vacation. There are so many beautiful places to enjoy the great outdoors; we couldn't possibly even touch the surface here. Here are a few choice family favorites. Grab the sunscreen and get outside!

Beaches

Cape Ann

Front and Back Beaches
Main Street, Rockport

These two tiny beaches are good for a short stint with small children. They're also a great place to go to skip stones in the water on cooler days. Limited metered public parking is available on the street, and there's a fairly clean public bathroom facility.

Good Harbor Beach

Thatcher Road, Gloucester
978-283-1601
Parking for non-residents is $20 on weekdays; $25, weekends and holidays.

Good Harbor is one of the best family beaches on the North Shore, with its soft sand, warm tidal pools for toddlers, and a great snack bar and bathroom set-up. There are plenty of showers to rinse off sand before getting in the car. Be sure to bring the camera for a shot of the kids running barefoot past the dunes along the boardwalk!

Long Beach

Route 127A, Gloucester/Rockport
There's a parking lot at 2 Beachland Avenue for non-residents: cost is $15 on weekdays.

Long Beach is a protected stretch of ocean and sand, which can also become very crowded on a hot summer day. But there's plenty of room for the kids to run around, especially at low tide. From Long Beach you can easily view the twin lighthouses on Thacher Island.

Niles Beach

Eastern Point Road, Gloucester

Parking is limited here, but for Gloucester residents who have a beach sticker it's an easy-access way to go to the beach. You can drive right up, park, and throw all of your beach gear over the wall. There are beautiful views of the harbor—you can see all the way to Boston on a clear day—and the beach is small enough that you won't lose track of small kids.

Pavilion Beach

Stacy Boulevard, Gloucester

This beach is a good diversion for kids if you're out and about in downtown Gloucester, walking along Stacy Boulevard, or getting an ice cream cone. Stop to skip a few stones in the water and enjoy views of the harbor.

Singing Beach

Off Route 127, Manchester-by-the-Sea
978-526-2019

Parking is extremely limited at Singing Beach unless you're a Manchester resident with a beach sticker. If you'd like to visit the beach, public transportation is encouraged. Guest fees/walk-on fees apply. The beach is very family-friendly, with a snack bar and restrooms.

 Bonfire on the Beach!

On summer Thursdays at 7PM, head to Salisbury Beach for an old-fashioned bonfire on the beach. Bring your beach chairs, blankets, family, and friends for marshmallow toasting and sing-alongs.

See www.beachfests.org for more information.

Stage Fort Park, Cressey's and Half Moon Beaches

Routes 133 & 127, Gloucester
978-281-8865
Parking fee is $10 on weekdays; $15, weekends and holidays.

This beautiful park overlooks Gloucester Harbor and features plenty of green space for picnics and a large playground with a rock climbing wall, a pirate ship, lighthouses, and a wooden truck that kids can pretend to drive. The Cupboard Restaurant is open seasonally and serves great, affordable meals. Half Moon and Cressey's beaches are two very small beaches just down the stairs from the gazebo—great for throwing stones in the water.

Wingaersheek Beach

Atlantic Street, Gloucester
978-283-1601
Parking fee for non-residents is $20 per car during the week; $25 on weekends. Parking is limited, so plan to arrive early.

Wingaersheek Beach is a great place for young kids, thanks to its warm tidal pools, big rocks to climb, and beautiful sand dunes. Since it's on

Ipswich Bay, the water is relatively calm and warm for the North Shore. The beach has a concession stand, restrooms, and showers. Bring your camera for a photo of the kids running down the wooden boardwalk.

Pavilion Beach
Stacy Boulevard, Gloucester

This beach is a good diversion for kids if you're out and about in downtown Gloucester, walking along Stacy Boulevard, or getting an ice cream cone. Stop to skip a few stones in the water and enjoy views of the harbor.

Greater Newburyport

Crane Beach
Argilla Road, Ipswich
978-356-4354 | www.thetrustees.org
Parking is $25 per car for non-members.

Crane Beach is widely regarded as one of the most beautiful beaches in the area, with its long stretches of white sand dotted with sand dunes. The beach is very family-friendly, with a snack shop, restrooms, and showers. The beach runs for miles and has beautiful sand dunes. Lifeguards are on duty during the beach season. Watch out for greenhead (biting horseflies) season toward the end of July to beginning of August!

Plum Island
Plum Island Turnpike, Newburyport
www.northofboston.org
$5 for cars, trucks, and motorcycles; $2 for bicycles.

Plum Island is a beautiful, family-friendly beach. Local families love the lighthouse, playground, and boardwalk and recommend plopping your towels down at Sandy Point, at the right end of the beach. You'll have to battle the crowds in the summer months, but the beach is quiet in the fall and winter months. Surf can sometimes be sizeable, and currents can get strong. The beach is closed in spring for piping plover nesting season. Note that there are no restrooms or snack bars available at the beach.

Also try:

Salisbury Beach State Reservation
Off Beach Road, Route 1A, Salisbury
978-462-4481 | www.mass.gov; Search: Salisbury Beach

Greater Salem

Lynch Park

Ober Street, off Route 127, Beverly
978-921-6067 | www.bevrec.com

Families will love Lynch Park for its sheer beauty and fun, open green space. The park and play structure overlooks the ocean, with paved paths for strollers and plenty of benches where you can soak up the sunshine.

Nahant Beach

Route 1A, Nahant
www.lynn-nahantbeach.org

This is a great beach for families; it is flat with very little surf, and the parking fee is only $3! At low tide the beach becomes shallow and long, so toddlers can run and splash to their hearts' content. The Tides restaurant, just over the Nahant causeway, is a great place to grab a bite to eat.

Also try:

Devereaux Beach
Ocean Avenue, Marblehead

Lynn Beach
Lynn Shore Drive, Lynn

Pearce Lake
Breakheart Reservation, 177 Forest Street, Saugus

Preston Beach
Atlantic Avenue, Marblehead/Swampscott

Spray Decks, Pools, and the Like

Cape Ann

Manchester Athletic Club (MAC)
8 Atwater Avenue, Manchester-by-the-Sea
978-526-8900 | www.manchesterathleticclub.com

A The MAC has a popular year-round indoor pool and hot tub, plus a seasonal outdoor pool with a play area and an outdoor café.

YMCA of the North Shore
Locations in Cape Ann, Beverly, Haverhill, Ipswich, Salem, and Marblehead
978-922-0990 | www.northshoreymca.org

A The Ys in Ipswich and Beverly are best known around the North Shore for their beautiful indoor pools, which always have space and open times for families to swim. In addition, Beverly has an outdoor pool, and moms boast that the outdoor pool in Marblehead is amazing—with big mushroom fountains and sprinklers that kids can operate on their own. Toddlers can walk right into the Marblehead pool, thanks to its L shape with a shallow end. Also worth a note: Marblehead's indoor pool has a big water slide, which is fun for kids in the winter months. The Y always has several lifeguards on duty, and kids generally need to be forty-two inches in height or be able to swim the length of the pool to swim without a bubble.

Greater Salem

Bradley Palmer Park Wading Pool
24 Asbury Street, Topsfield
978-468-1938 | www.massparks.org

Bradley Palmer has a great wading pool for toddlers with a spraying mushroom. There are also bathroom facilities and a small playground right next to the pool. Note that there's an entrance fee of $5 per car to enter the park.

Patton Park

340 Bay Road, Hamilton
978-468-2178 | hamiltonma.virtualtownhall.net
Daily in the summer, 11:30AM–6PM.
Family pool pass is $95 for the season. Non-member fee is $3 per day per person ($10 max per family).

Patton Park has a great swim program for kids, including swimming lessons, swim team, and a summer camp where kids swim in the pool daily.

Paul J. Lydon Aquatic Center

200 Commonwealth Avenue, Danvers
978-774-9335 | www.massparks.org

The Lydon Aquatic Center is an affordable, family-friendly, family-run center. Moms rave about their swim lessons. They even offer kayak lessons for kids in the pool!

Pleasant Pond and Beach

Pleasant Street, Wenham
978-468-5520 | www.wehnhamma.gov

Pleasant Pond Beach is the only public swimming site in Wenham. The beach is available to residents for swimming, aquatic activities, fishing, and boating. Each spring, the state stocks the pond with trout, making it a popular fishing spot as well. Alas, in recent years, swimming has been limited because of problems with weed control and occasional high levels of bacteria. The beach has also not had lifeguards for the past few years, due to budget issues. A group of residents recently came together to form the Pleasant Pond Neighborhood Association, to help maintain Pleasant Pond. The group is exploring non-profit status and has developed a master plan for the area. Stay tuned!

Merrimack Valley

Geisler Memorial Swimming Pool

50 High Street, Lawrence

978-687-1024 | www.mass.gov; Search: Geisler Swimming Pool
Monday–Friday, 10AM–7PM; weekends, 11AM–7PM.
Free.

Geisler Memorial Swimming Pool has a Learn to Swim program that runs on Monday and Friday mornings, plus open swim from noon to 7PM daily.

Lt. Colonel Edward J. Higgins Swimming Pool
Crawford Street, Lawrence
978-687-0393 | www.mass.gov; Search: Higgins Swimming Pool
Monday–Friday, 10AM–7PM; weekends, 11AM–7PM.
Free.

This pool has a Learn to Swim program from 10AM to 11AM weekdays, and open swim daily from 10AM to 7PM.

Pomps Pond
Located off of Abbot Street, Andover
978-623-8274 | www.andoverma.gov; Search: Pomps Pond
Andover residents can purchase a season pass for $100 per car. Non-residents, $5 per person per day.

Pomps Pond offers a sunbathing area; recreational swimming; shaded picnic grounds; a children's playground area including a volleyball net; sailboat, canoe, and kayak rentals; bathrooms; showers; and a concession stand. Sunday afternoon Family Fun Days include a family splash party with sandcastle building and the Annual Rotten Sneaker Contest. (Bet *that* piqued your interest!)

Stevens Pond
Pleasant Street, North Andover
978-682-9000 | www.nayouth.com/stevens-pond.html
Residents can purchase a season pass for $75. Adult day passes for guests of residents and residents without stickers can be purchased for $12 per adult (a daily fee); children are free when accompanied by a paying adult.

Stevens Pond is a fun place for kids to swim in the summer. There's a bath house and a playground on the premises, as well as a concession stand.

There's a roped-off area for swimming, with certified lifeguards on duty, and a dock that bigger kids can swim out to.

Getting on the Water

Whether you're an old salt or a landlubber, here are a few family-friendly boating events and adventures that you won't want to miss!

Cape Ann

Race to the Bottom
Back Beach, Rockport
Race organizer can be reached at 978-546-6788

Race to the Bottom is a fun, family-friendly fundraiser that usually takes place in mid-July. Teams—who pay $100 to participate—are given two hours to assemble a cardboard boat to race around buoys and back to shore. Materials used by these intrepid teams include two four-by-eight-foot sheets of cardboard, some wood strapping, a giant roll of duct tape, one can of spray shellac, a yardstick, a knife, and a rope. Awards are given out for the top three finishers, the best designed boat, the most outrageous boat, and the first boat to sink. Proceeds go to several local charities. Hot dogs and beverages are usually sold at the event.

The Schooner Thomas E. Lannon
Seven Seas Wharf, Rogers Street, Gloucester
978-281-6634 | www.schooner.org

The sixty-five-foot wooden schooner sails out of Gloucester Harbor. You can learn about the inner workings of the ship or just sit back and enjoy the view.

Greater Salem

Rubber Duck Regatta
Redd's Pond, Marblehead

The Marblehead Rotary Club hosts an annual event at Redd's Pond. For five dollars, participants race rubber ducks across the pond. Five hundred dollars goes to the first place winner; $250 for second place; and $100 for third place. All proceeds benefit the Rotary Scholarship Fund.

Camping & Canoeing

Cape Ann

Cape Ann Camp Site
80 Atlantic Street, Gloucester
978-283-8683 | www.capeanncampsite.net
$30–$36 base rate per car, up to two people; $8 per additional adult and $2 per additional child up to sixteen years old.

Whether you have an RV and would like a full hookup site or you just want to pitch a tent, Cape Ann Camp Site has a spot for your family. Every site comes with a ready-made fireplace and picnic table. There are also six toilet and shower buildings, plus a small campsite store stocked with ice and wood. There's even a centrally located wireless Internet signal for those who just aren't that into nature.

Little River Campground
4 Stanwood Point, Gloucester
978-283-2616
Tent sites are $35 per day or $200 per week.

The Little River Campground has a unique blend of ocean and wooded countryside, offering swimming at a private swimming area, kayaking, boating, fishing, diving, and more. Cottage rentals (some waterfront) and campsites are available for rent.

Greater Newburyport

Foote Brothers Canoe Rentals
230 Topsfield Road, Ipswich, at Willowdale Dam on the Ipswich River
978-356-9771 | www.footebrotherscanoes.com
For a little inexpensive fun, rent a canoe and paddle up the Ipswich River.

The Pines Camping Area
28 CCC Road, Salisbury
978-465-0013 | www.pinescampingarea.com
Mid-April–October.

No-frills woodland family camping, one and a half miles to the ocean.

Salisbury Beach State Reservation
Off Beach Road, Route 1A, Salisbury
978-462-4481 | www.mass.gov; Search: Salisbury Beach

Salisbury Beach State Reservation is a five-hundred-twenty-acre beach bordered by the Atlantic and the Merrimack River. The beach has a playground, restrooms, shower, and changing areas.

Playgrounds, Parks, Picnic Spots & Green Spaces

Cape Ann

Coolidge Reservation
15 Coolidge Point, Manchester-by-the-Sea
978-526-8687 | www.thetrustees.org
Year-round, daily, 8AM–sunset.

The Coolidge Reservation is a Trustees of Reservations property. It's a beautiful place to go walking or hiking any time of year. Bring a blanket, a picnic, and a Frisbee or soccer ball and take the family out to the Ocean Lawn (open year-round, Friday–Monday, 8AM–sunset), for some beautiful wide-open playspaces and spectacular ocean views.

Essex Elementary School Eagles Nest Playground

12 Story Street, Essex
978-768-7324 | www.essexel.mersd.org

The Eagles Nest Playground at the Essex Elementary School is a local favorite, thanks to its enormous wooden climbing structure with tons of nooks and crannies. Kids can play for hours, as long as school's not in session. Kids will also love the pond and may spot a bull frog or two. There are also basketball courts and plenty of parking in the school parking lot when school's out.

Masconomo Park

Beach Street, Manchester-by-the-Sea
978-526-2019 | www.manchester.ma.us

Masconomo Park has a beautiful little playground that's perfect for smaller kids. There's a separate play structure for toddlers and preschoolers, plus a baseball diamond/soccer field, and a portable restroom. Moms will love to sit on the benches and take in the beautiful ocean views while kids play.

Rockport Elementary School Playground

34 Jerden's Lane, Rockport
978-546-1200

The Rockport Elementary School has a beautiful, brand-new play structure that kids and adults alike will love. There are plenty of places to climb, run, and slide. There's also a wide-open grassy field for kicking around a soccer ball or flying a kite.

The Science Playground at West Parish Elementary School

10 Concord Street, Gloucester
978-281-9835 | www.gloucesterschools.com

The Science Playground at West Parish Elementary School in Gloucester is funded primarily by grants from the National Science Foundation, the Massachusetts Institute of Technology (MIT), and by PTO fundraising. The playground, which was built by parent volunteers and MIT professors, is in the shape of a giant ship and features some fun hands-on science components, including surge swings, pulley systems, organ pipes, and more.

Stage Fort Park
Hough Avenue, Gloucester
978-281-8865 | www.essexheritage.org; Search: Stage Fort Park

Stage Fort Park has something for everyone, with its beautiful ocean views, rolling green lawn, and fun play structures. There's an older playground reminiscent of mom's childhood and a new state-of-the-art playground complete with a lighthouse, a wooden truck, and a rock climbing wall. You'll also find plenty of benches and picnic tables. The parking lot is for residents only, but there is plenty of metered parking along Stacy Boulevard.

Tuck's Point
17 Tuck's Point Road, Manchester-by-the-Sea
978-526-2019 | www.manchester.ma.us

Tuck's Point is a beautiful place to spend the day as a family. There's a playground, plus a small beach, a picnic area, and bathroom facilities. The Chowder House and Rotunda can be rented for group functions.

Greater Newburyport

Action Cove
15 Bachelor Street, West Newbury

This playground has an amazing climbing structure, newly updated with plastic caps and timbers on all railings and flooring of the wooden structure. There are tons of nooks, crannies, and platforms to keep your kids entertained, as well as nearby ball fields. It's a great place to meet other moms, or to have an impromptu play date.

Amesbury Sports Park
12 South Hunt Road, Amesbury
978-388-5788 | www.amesburysportspark.net
Summers, Saturday and Sunday, 10AM–7PM.

The sports park features big hills and big thrills, including summer tubing and the OGO, an eleven-foot transparent plastic ball that lets you jump inside and roll down a hill.

Inn Street Playground
Downtown Newburyport

The Inn Street Playground is a hotspot with the stroller set in Newburyport. Many moms will hit the Starbucks in Market Square, then stroll on over to the playground, which is perfect for toddlers and young kids who will love to splash in the fountains on a hot day.

Moseley Woods
14 Spofford Street, Newburyport
www.moseleywoods.com

Moseley Woods is a nice place to bring little ones for a picnic. There's a pavilion and a waterfront where kids can throw rocks in the water and watch the boats go by. The bathroom facilities are nice, and there's even a zipline for the bigger kids.

Sawyer's Island
Patmos Road, Rowley
978-768-7241 | www.ecga.org; Search: Sawyer's Island

Sawyer's Island is a beautiful place to picnic under the oak and hickory trees and enjoy views of Plum Island Sound. Getting to Sawyer's Island requires a very pretty mile-long walk. See the website for directions.

Greater Salem

Endicott Park
57 Forest Street, Danvers
978-774-6518
www.danversrec.com/endicott
$1 per car for residents; $3 per car for non-residents.

Endicott Park is great for small kids with its huge playground and outdoor farm animals such as horses, sheep, and chickens. There's a beautiful green space for picnics, or just for letting the little ones roam wild.

Glen Meadow Park
Trickett Road, Lynnfield

Glen Meadow is a nice place to take smaller kids, since they have a separate toddler play structure and a sandbox, plus plenty of green space for kicking around a ball or having a picnic.

Ipswich River Wildlife Sanctuary
87 Perkins Row, Topsfield
978-887-9264 | www.massaudubon.org
Tuesday–Sunday, and Monday holidays, sunrise to sunset.
Non-member adults, $4; non-member children (ages three to twelve) and seniors, $3.

Put the baby in the backpack for a stroll down the boardwalk, where you'll hear bull frogs and spot snapping turtles. The surrounding forest is home to owls, wild turkeys, woodpeckers, hummingbirds, and warblers. Kids can take classes to learn about everything from bugs and birds to maple sugaring. Moms rave about Fairy Day, when kids read stories and build fairy houses.

Long Hill
572 Essex Street, Beverly
978-921-1944 | www.thetrustees.org
Year-round, daily, 8AM–5PM.
Free.

The Long Hill Horticulture Center offers botanically inspired, hands-on workshops, in-depth garden tours, and a range of garden programs and events for adults, children, and families. Stroll through five acres of gardens, which are laid out in a series of rooms surrounding a federal style house. Don't miss the Children's Garden, where kids can feel free to get their hands dirty. Long Hill also has seasonal pick-your-own vegetables and flowers.

Merrimack Valley

Drummond Playground
Johnson and Milk streets, North Andover

This is a popular playground for preschoolers, with its nice wooden structure featuring swings, tire swings, slides, a hanging bridge, and climbing ropes. There are wooden benches and picnic tables, and a nice lawn. The playground is fenced on three sides and there are nearby athletic fields.

Stevens-Coolidge Place
137 Andover Street, North Andover
978-682-3580 | www.thetrustees.org
Year-round, daily, 8AM–sunset.
Free; on-site donation welcome from non-members.

Take the family on a stroll through the perennial gardens, through a kitchen and cut flower garden, a rose garden, a French potager garden, and a greenhouse complex, all surrounded by woods, orchards, and hay fields. Gardens are most vibrant mid-June–September.

Veasey Memorial Park
201 Washington Street, Groveland
978-521-9345 | www.veaseypark.org

Bring the family for a picnic on top of the hill overlooking Johnson Pond.

State Parks

Cape Ann

Halibut Point State Park
Gott Avenue, Rockport

978-546-2997 | www.massparks.org
Memorial Day–Labor Day, daily, 8AM–8PM. A parking fee is charged.

Halibut Point has seventy-three acres of beautiful walking trails. Spectacular scenic spots look out over the ocean, where you can see Crane Beach, the Merrimack River, the Isle of Shoals in New Hampshire and even Mount Agamenticus in Maine. There's a lighthouse for small children to climb, as well as a quarry to walk around. It's a beautiful place for a picnic.

Greater Newburyport

Maudslay State Park
Curzon Mill Road, Newburyport
978-456-7223 | www.essexheritage.org
Year-round, 8:30AM–4PM.
Admission is free; parking is $2.

Maudslay State Park has 480 beautiful acres of meadows, gardens, and trails for hiking, walking, and biking. You may just spot a bald eagle nesting in the white pines along the Merrimack River. The Maudslay Arts Center also has a summer concert series; bring a blanket for the lawn seating.

Plum Island State Reservation
Plum Island, Northern Boulevard, Newburyport
978-465-5753 | www.newburyportchamber.org

Plum Island has miles of beautiful sandy beaches and a national wildlife refuge, offering plenty of bird watching opportunities. Parking is available (for a fee) at the refuge, the point, or in private parking lots.

Salisbury Beach State Reservation
Off Beach Road, Route 1A, Salisbury
978-462-4481 | www.massparks.org

Salisbury Beach State Reservation has 520 acres with 484 campsites and beach access. The park offers swimming, boating, fishing, and camping and is very popular with trailer campers. Facilities include the campground, with renovated bathhouses, an extensive day-use parking lot, restroom facilities, and a new playground and pavilion area.

Sandy Point State Reservation
Parker River Wildlife Refuge, Ipswich
978-462-4481 | www.massparks.org

Sandy Point is at the very southern tip of Plum Island. The park is seventy-seven acres set amid the state's most beautiful and popular coastal beaches. The reservation is open sunrise till sunset, and parking is allowed in two designated areas, which fill up quickly.

Willowdale State Forest
Linebrook Road, Ipswich
978-887-5931 | www.massparks.org

Willowdale has forty miles of trails for hiking, horseback riding, mountain biking, cross-country skiing, and walking.

Greater Salem

Bradley Palmer State Park
Asbury Street, Topsfield
978-887-5931 | www.massparks.org
$5 per car to use the wading pool.

Bradley Palmer is a great spot for kids and adults alike in any season, with over forty miles of trails, including hiking and walking trails, equestrian trails, paved bike paths, and mountain bike trails. Near the south gate, you'll find picnic tables and a wading pool with a giant mushroom fountain that's perfect for the infant-to-six-years group. There's also a nearby playground and grassy area for picnics, plus restrooms. Adults will love the views of the Ipswich River.

Merrimack Valley

Georgetown-Rowley State Forest
Route 97, Georgetown
978-887-5931 | www.massparks.org

This state park has 1,124 acres for hiking, walking, horseback riding, cross-country skiing, and more.

Harold Parker State Forest
1951 Turnpike Street/Route 114, North Andover
978-686-3391 | www.massparks.org
Year-round.
Free.

The Harold Parker State Forest has eleven ponds and three thousand acres of pine forest, offering plenty of opportunities for canoeing, fishing, kayaking, hiking, biking, swimming, and more.

Lawrence Heritage State Park
1 Jackson Street, Lawrence
978-794-1655 | www.massparks.org

The Lawrence Heritage State Park has one hundred twenty-one acres of walking trails and paved bike paths, perfect for strollers and family bike rides. Check out the visitor's center, which details the life of the nineteenth-century mill town.

Lawrence Riverfront State Park
Eaton and Everett Streets, Lawrence
978-681-8675 | www.massparks.org

The Lawrence Riverfront State Park offers tennis, basketball, and street hockey courts; wooded walking trails; a children's play area; and a great sledding hill. Keep in mind, sailing lessons are available for children nine years and up through Greater Lawrence Community Boating.

Biking and Hiking Trails and Paths

Cape Ann

Choate Island (Hog Island)
Essex River Estuary, Essex
978-356-4351 | www.ttor.org
Year-round, 8AM–4PM.

Choate Island can only be accessed by private boat, kayak, or a guided tour. Once there, you'll find panoramic views of the marshes, estuary, and ocean, plus a dark spruce forest. See what your eagle-eyed tot can spot in this birder's paradise!

Cox Reservation
82 Eastern Avenue, Route 133, Essex
978-768-7241 | www.essexheritage.org; Search: Cox Reservation

The Cox Reservation, owned by the Essex County Greenbelt Association, is a beautiful place for walking, hiking, or cross-country skiing, with twenty-seven acres of salt marsh and farmland. The views of the Essex River, the salt marsh, Crane Beach, and Castle Hill are stunning. Art lovers won't want to miss the annual Art in the Barn event that takes place each June.

Dogtown Common
Cherry Street, Gloucester/Rockport

Dogtown is an abandoned settlement in the center of Cape Ann known for its woods, giant boulders, and rock formations. You'll find miles of trails for biking, hiking, walking, and cross-country skiing. Look for boulders carved with inspirational messages carved by unemployed Finnish quarry workers during the Great Depression. You'll want to pick up a trail map in advance from the Gloucester Office of Tourism, located at 9 Dale Avenue in Gloucester.

A to Z List of Hiking and Biking Trails

Amesbury Riverwalk, Amesbury

Appleton Farms & Grass Ride, Ipswich

Bradley Palmer State Park, Topsfield

Dogtown Common, Gloucester/Rockport

Eastern Marsh Rail Trail, Salisbury

Essex County Greenbelt/Cox Reservation, Essex (hiking only)

Georgetown-Rowley State Forest, Georgetown

Halibut Point State Park, Rockport (hiking only)

Harold Parker State Forest, North Andover

Lawrence Heritage State Park, Lawrence (hiking only)

Lynn Beach, Lynn

Lynn Woods, Lynn

Maudslay State Park, Newburyport (hiking only)

Old Town Hill, Newbury (hiking only)

Parker River National Wildlife Refuge, Plum Island

Ravenswood Park, Gloucester

Salem-Marblehead Rail Trail (biking only)

Salem Willows Park, Salem

Salisbury Beach Reservation, Salisbury

Stage Fort Park, Gloucester

Ward Reservation, North Andover (hiking only)

Willowdale State Forest, Ipswich

Source: North of Boston Visitor's Guide

Ravenswood Park

Western Avenue/Route 127, Gloucester
978-526-8687 | www.thetrustees.org
Entrance to the park is free; parking is limited.

If you want to impart a sense of wonder in your children, Ravenswood Park is a beautiful place to take the family for a quiet walk through the woods. (It's also a great place to take the dog for a walk on your own!) In the winter, you'll find great trails for cross-country skiing and snowshoeing. Don't miss the view overlooking Gloucester Harbor and the hike through Great Magnolia Swamp. Also make sure you check out the Hermit's Haven Question, a wonderful treasure hunt through the trails.

Greater Newburyport

Appleton Farms & Grass Rides

219 County Road, Ipswich
978-356-5728 | www.ttor.org
Year-round, sunrise–sunset.
Free for members of the Trustees of Reservations; non-members, $3.

Appleton Farms is one of the oldest continuously operating farms in the country. The Grass Rides (grass covered avenues), which were established by the Appleton family as horseback riding trails, extend through five miles of beautiful woods. From the air, the trails fan out in the shape of a wagon wheel, with five paths converging at a single point. Green dogs permit required to walk dogs. Mountain biking is permitted only on designated trails May 1–February 28; trails are closed to mountain bikes March 1–April 30, during the muddy season. Try out one of the family-friendly quests. Pick up your copy at the bulletin boards located in any of the parking lots.

Clipper City Rail Trail

www.cityofnewburyport.com; Search: Clipper City

The Clipper City Rail Trail is a new 1.1-mile trail between the Merrimack River and the MBTA Commuter Rail Station. The paved path is great for strollers and bikes, with water views along the entire path. You'll also find artwork and sculpture along the trail, plus plenty of opportunities to rest or grab a bite to eat. After your walk, be sure to stop at Haley's Ice Cream or Cashman Park playground.

Coastal Trails Coalition

PO Box 1016, Newburyport
www.coastaltrails.org

The Coastal Trails Coalition (CTC) is an all-volunteer, non-profit organization whose mission is to assist in the development, promotion, and stewardship of the Coastal Trails Network, a thirty-mile public system of bicycle and pedestrian trails connecting the communities of Amesbury, Newbury, Newburyport, and Salisbury. The goal is to link unique coastal features, town centers, neighborhoods, and transportation hubs. For some great information about area trail entrances and parking around trails, visit the website.

Crane Wildlife Refuge

Argilla Road, Ipswich
978-412-2557 | www.ttor.org
Year-round, 8AM–sunset.

At the Crane Wildlife Refuge, you'll find beach, forest, and dunes, all with breathtaking views of Ipswich Bay. Watch for their annual sand sculpture competition—it's fun for the whole family, and spectators are welcome with regular beach admission.

Greenwood Farm

Jeffrey's Neck Road, Ipswich
978-356-4351 | www.thetrustees.org
Year-round, sunrise to sunset.

Greenwood Farm has beautiful hiking, walking, or cross-country skiing trails, where you might spot egrets, great blue herons, swallows, bobolinks, and red spot in the marshes. Note that dogs must be leashed.

Hamlin Reservation
Argilla Road, Ipswich
978-356-4351 | www.ttor.org
Year-round, sunrise to sunset.

The Hamlin Reservation is a beautiful hiking, birding, and cross-country skiing spot with forests and plenty of wildlife. There is a one-mile loop trail to Eagle Island, which provides moderate walking. Note that dogs are not allowed.

Hood Pond
Willowdale State Forest, Linebrook Road, Ipswich
978-887-5931 | www.ipswichma.com

This hundred-acre pond, located within the Willowdale State Forest, is home to a rare species of butterfly nests in the tops of the white cedars. Bog lemmings can sometimes be seen in the swamps.

Maudslay State Park
Curzon Mill Road, Newburyport
978-456-7223 | www.essexheritage.org
Year-round, 8:30AM–4PM.
Admission is free; parking is $2.

Maudslay State Park has beautiful nineteenth-century gardens, plus trails for biking, hiking, horseback riding, cross-country skiing, and snowshoeing. It's a beautiful place to take the family for a picnic.

Old Town Hill
Newman Road, Newbury
978-356-4351 | www.ttor.org

This stunning location offers scenic vistas (you'll be able to see three states from the peak of Old Town Hill!), amazing bird watching (watch for egrets and great blue herons), and stunning views of marshes and tidal creeks. Great for hiking, walking, fishing, kayaking, and cross-country skiing.

Powow Riverwalk

The trail starts on Water Street in the Lower Mills district
of downtown Amesbury.
978-388-3178 | www.amesburychamber.com

This 1.3-mile rail trail along the Powow River has a paved asphalt surface,
which makes it great for bikes and strollers. There's free parking in downtown
Amesbury, at the Water Street Town Parking Garage.

Greater Salem

Breakheart Reservation

Forest Street, Saugus
781-233-0834 | www.saugus.org/FOBR

Breakheart's Pearce Lake offers one of the few fresh water swimming
spots north of Boston. You'll also find a wonderful network of trails for
hiking, walking, and biking.

Lynn Shores and Nahant Beach Reservation

Lynn Shore Drive/Nahant Beach Boulevard, Lynn
781-485-2803 | www.massparks.org
Year-round, sunrise to sunset.

A good two-mile walk along the promenade, with views of Lynn Harbor and
Nahant Bay the entire way. You'll find four beaches, including Kings Beach,
Lynn Beach, Nahant Beach, and Long Beach. Includes a saltwater beach
and walking trails. Don't miss the tide pools at Red Rock Park, which are
often filled with marine life.

Lynn Woods

Pennybrook Road, Lynn
781-477-7123 | www.essexheritage.org

As the second-largest municipal park in the United States, Lynn Woods
offers thirty miles of trails through forest, wetlands, ponds, and streams.
A climb to the top of the Stone Tower offers views of Lynn's waterfront,
Boston, and more. Bring a blanket and pack a picnic for a stop in the Lynn
Woods Rose Garden or on top of Burrill Hill or Mt. Gilead.

Merrimack Valley

Deer Jump Reservation
River Road, Andover
978-659-2697 | www.avisandover.org

The Deer Jump Reservation has beautiful hiking, walking, and cross-country skiing, with high bluffs offering views of the Merrimack River.

Den Rock Park
Route 114, Lawrence
978-974-0770 | www.andovertrails.org

This is one of the most popular places in Essex County for outdoor rock climbing. On a hike through the 120-acre park, you may come across wildlife as diverse as deer, coyotes, fox, beaver, redtail hawks, great blue herons, and kingfishers.

Goldsmith Woodlands
491 South Main Street (Route 28), Andover
978-996-4475 | www.avisandover.org

Put the baby in the backpack for a hike in the woodlands, which feature black pines, marshes of cattails, and views of Foster's Pond.

Harold Parker State Forest, North Andover
305 Middleton Road, North Andover
978-686-3391 | www.mass.gov/dcr

Harold Parker State Forest offers hiking, mountain biking, fishing, horseback riding, camping, and picnicking. There are accessible beaches, plus places for camping and canoeing.

Ward Reservation
Prospect Road, Andover
978-682-3580 | www.ttor.org
Year-round, daily, 8AM–sunset.

Hike to the top of Holt Hill, the highest point in Essex County, for views of the Boston skyline. You'll find thirteen miles of trails and seventeen miles of stone walls. Follow the numbered stations along the nature trail to explore Pine Hole Bog, a rare quaking bog with distinct vegetation. Allow a minimum of two hours.

Weir Hill
Stevens Street, North Andover
978-682-3580 | www.ttor.org

Hike, bike, or cross-country ski through these sixty acres of forest, with intermittent streams and wet meadows. Skip the stroller and put the baby in a backpack or carrier.

Farms and Petting Zoos

Greater Newburyport

Appleton Farms & Grass Rides
219 County Road, Ipswich
978-356-5728 | www.ttor.org
Year-round, sunrise to sunset.
Free for members of the Trustees of Reservations; non-members, $3.

Appleton Farms is one of the oldest continuously operating farms in the country. The Grass Rides (grass covered avenues), which were established by the Appleton family as horseback riding trails, extend through five miles of beautiful woods. From the air, the trails fan out in the shape of a wagon wheel, with five paths converging at a single point. Green dogs permit required to walk dogs. Mountain biking is permitted only on designated trails May 1–February 28; trails are closed to mountain bikes March 1–April 30, during the muddy season.

Cider Hill Farm
45 Fern Avenue, Amesbury
978-388-5525 | www.ciderhill.com

Cider Hill Farm is a great place to go for a walk through the orchards. The farm has hayrides and pick-your-own peaches, apples, or pumpkins. During apple-picking season, you'll love their award-winning cider donuts and mulled apple cider. You can also view a working bee colony, complete with its queen. The livestock pen is open for viewing and is always a treat for the little ones, with goats, turkeys, chickens, and other farm animals.

Long Hill Orchard and Farm

520 Main Street, West Newbury
978-363-2170 | www.longhillorchard.com

Small kids will love the petting zoo of miniature goats and chickens. The farm has free hayrides on weekends and Haunted Halloween Hayrides throughout October ($10 per person; children under two, free). You can pick your own apples, peaches, and pears seasonally, or visit the farm stand, which sells fresh produce, baked goods, and ice cream. The farm also offers a vegetable CSA (community-supported agriculture) program.

Marini Farm

259 Linebrook Road, Ipswich
978-356-0430 | www.marinifarm.com
See website for hours of operation and seasonal offerings.

Marini Farm in Ipswich has been voted the best farm in New England by New England Cable Network viewers, and it truly is a farm for all seasons. The farm holds a strawberry festival in June, complete with hayrides, ice cream, strawberry shortcake, and a jumping pillow and other inflatables. Christmas on the Hill features giant snowmen and free hot chocolate. The farm also has a corn maze, a farm stand, and a greenhouse for annuals, herbs, vegetables, perennials, and more.

Morehouse's Wheeler Brook Farm

57 Jewett Street, Georgetown
978-352-8289 | www.wheelerbrookfarm.net
Daily during the harvest season.

Morehouse's Wheeler Brook Farm is a place where small kids can play and learn. Visit with farm animals, swings, and a Penny Heaven sandbox, where young archaeologists can dig for treasure. The farm has seasonal pick-your-own strawberries, blueberries, raspberries, and rhubarb, plus some veggies like peas, beets, green and yellow beans, lettuce, cabbage, tomatoes, and spinach. The farm stand has fresh produce and cut flowers.

Russell Orchards
143 Argilla Road, Ipswich
978-356-5366 | www.russellorchards.com
Daily, May–November.

This is a great place for kids and adults alike. Go for blueberry and straw-berry picking in the summer and apple picking in the fall. Kids will love the petting zoo, playground, and hayrides. Adults will love the bakery, winery, and fresh produce. Kids can watch apple cider presses in the works, and adults can snap some great holiday photos of kids in the fall pumpkin patch! Don't miss the apple cider donuts.

Tendercrop Farm
108 High Road, Newbury
978-462-6972 | www.tendercropfarms.com

Tendercrop Farm is a good place to go to buy local produce, chicken, beef, and baked goods. Kids will love the strawberry and blueberry picking. Across the street, you'll find Little Farm, where kids can get up close and personal with animals like turkeys, sheep, and horses.

Wolf Hollow
114 Essex Road, Ipswich
978-356-0216 | www.wolfhollowipswich.org
See website for hours of operation, which vary by season.

Wolf Hollow is a non-profit organization that teaches people about the importance of the wolf in the wild. In its one-hour educational lecture, Wolf Hollow offers the opportunity to view gray wolves in as natural a setting as possible. The program is recommended for kids five and up. All visitors are invited to howl with the wolves at the end of each presentation.

Woodsom Farm
222 Lion's Mouth Road, Amesbury
978-388-8562
Year-round, sunrise to sunset.

At one time, this was the largest dairy farm in Essex County. Today, the Woodsom Farm annual festival features arts and crafts, pumpkin carving and decorating, bounce houses, hayrides, a petting farm, pony rides, live entertainment, contests, and more.

Greater Salem

Brooksby Farm
54 Felton Street, Peabody
978-531-7456 | www.brooksbyfarm.org
Daily, 9AM–5PM.

Brooksby Farm is a fun place to visit year-round. You can pick your own fruits and veggies through the summer and fall—you'll even find winter squash in December. The bakery has delicious cider donuts, hot mulled cider, cold cider, and coffee, plus homemade pies and gifts available for purchase. Kids will love visiting the barnyard animals. And don't forget the hayrides on the weekends during apple-picking season.

Connors Farm

30 Valley Road (Route 35), Danvers
978-777-1245 | www.connorsfarm.com
Daily, 9AM–6PM.

There's so much to do at Connors Farm that it might just take your breath away. Families can pick their own fruits and veggies, wind their way through the corn maze, chase their kids around as they attack a giant jumping pillow or bouncy house, race toy ducks, take a hayride, scurry through a mini maze, and much, much more. From pony rides to a hay jump, Connors Farm is a great place to visit. The farm also has a market and bakery, a CSA (community-supported agriculture) program, and an annual strawberry festival in the summer.

Green Meadows Farm

656 Asbury Street, Hamilton
978-468-2277 | www.gmfarm.com
See website for hours, which vary by season.

Green Meadows is a great place to stock up on organic fruits and veggies, cheese, meat, and fish, as they're a certified organic farm with a CSA (community-supported agriculture) program and a CSF (community-supported fisheries) program. Through the farm's education programs, kids can get exposure to real farm life. Their Little Farmers program, for kids ages three to five with a parent, introduces kids to livestock raised on the farm. The class does up-close watering and feeding, plus hands-on activities, stories, and songs. (Cost is $40 per session.) The farm also holds a blueberry and strawberry festival in the summer, as well as a corn and harvest festival in the fall.

Myopia Hunt Club

435 Bay Road, South Hamilton

978-468-4433 | www.myopiahunt.com

Here's something truly unique to the North Shore: the Myopia Hunt Club. In the fall, the Club has fox hunts that are open to the public. Kids will love the see the horses and hounds. Sunday polo matches are also open to the public—kids can sit alongside the field and watch the horses thunder by.

Merrimack Valley

Boston Hill Farm
Route 114, North Andover
978-681-8556 | www.bostonhillfarm.com
Year-round, 9AM–7PM.

At Boston Hill Farm, kids can hand-feed the sheep and goats in the petting zoo or they can visit the chickens, geese, bunnies, and calves. The farm also has pumpkin and apple picking, and hayrides for little ones with tired feet. Don't miss the bakery, or the Richardson's ice cream!

Mann Orchards, Inc.
27 Pleasant Valley Street, Methuen
978-683-0361 | www.mannorchards.com

Mann Orchards is a great place to stock up on fresh produce. You'll also find great pies, cider donuts, and marinated meats.

Smolak Farms
315 South Bradford Street, North Andover
978-682-6332 | www.smolakfarms.com

Families love Smolak Farms for their beautiful orchards and berry fields. Smaller children will love the playground, the wee wagon rides, the duck races, and seeing animals like deer, llamas, sheep, and chickens. Their strawberry and peach festivals are very popular, as are their apple and berry picking seasons. There's a great summer nature and craft program for older kids. Don't forget to hit the bakery for some great seasonal fruit pies—yum!

Tattersall Farm

542 North Broadway, Haverhill
www.tattersallfarm.org
Daily, sunrise to sunset.

The Tattersall Farm has working hayfields, meadows, and beautiful wooded paths for walking, jogging, and cross-country skiing. The trails take you through the woods, hayfields, meadows, and past historic farm buildings.

Turkey Hill Farm

380 Middle Road, Haverhill
978-372-9474 | www.turkeyhillfarm.com

You'll love Turkey Hill Farm for their strawberry and blueberry picking, and for the chance to cut down your own Christmas tree in November and December.

More North Shore Farms & Petting Zoos:

- Barker's Farm Stand, North Andover
- Brick House Farm, Newbury
- Clark Farm, Danvers
- Farmer Brown's, Middleton
- Homestead Farm & Orchard, Merrimac
- Ingraham Christmas Tree Farm, Georgetown
- Rogers Spring Hill Farm, Haverhill

Outdoor Education

Cape Ann

Cape Ann Discovery Center at Ravenswood Park

Western Avenue (Route 127), Gloucester
978-526-8687 | www.thetrustees.org

If you're going to Ravenswood Park, make sure you stop at the Cape Ann Discovery Center, just by the entrance. It's a great little spot where kids can experiment with microscopes and learn more about nature and wildlife. Check out the bulletin board to find a copy of the "Hermit's Haven Quest." Although geared toward older kids, this treasure hunt is sure to provide a little extra excitement.

Greater Newburyport

Joppa Flats Education Center and Wildlife Sanctuary
1 Plum Island Turnpike, Newburyport
978-462-9998
www.massaudubon.org

This is a great spot for beginning and experienced bird watchers of all ages—you'll spot seasonal songbirds, shorebirds, and waterfowl, birds, butterflies, and beautiful vistas.

The Parker River National Wildlife Refuge
6 Plum Island Turnpike, Newburyport
978-465-5753 | www.fws.gov/northeast/parkerriver
Year-round, sunrise to sunset. Subject to temporary closures due to weather, crowds, or special events.

Entrance fee of $5 per car or $2 per walk or bike on.
Annual passes available for $20.

This is one of the country's most productive, year-round wildlife viewing areas, boasting over three hundred species of birds. There are plenty of hands-on exhibits to keep the kids busy, not to mention miles of sand dunes, beaches, marshes, and mud flats. Take note: restrooms do not have running water from late fall through winter, and pets are not allowed.

Plum Island Estuary

www.newburyportchamber.org; Search: Plum Island

Take the family and a pair of binoculars for a day of bird watching. Also worth checking out is the Joppa Flats Education Center. (See page 150.)

Merrimack Valley

Harlan P. Kelsey Arboretum

18 Kelsey Road, Boxford
978-561-5611 | www.essexheritage.org
Year-round, dawn to dusk.
Free.

This beautiful four-and-a-half-acre arboretum featuring ornamental trees and shrubs is just two miles from downtown Georgetown. The arboretum is especially worth a visit from early April through July, when everything is abloom!

Maritime Events and Activities

Cape Ann

Adventures at Yankee Whale Watching and Deep Sea Fishing

PO Box 1325, Gloucester
978-283-0313 | www.yankeefleet.com

Grab the kids and hit the high seas. Whale sightings are guaranteed and trips are narrated.

A Cape Ann Whale Watch

415 Main Street, Rose Wharf, Gloucester
978-283-5110 | www.seethewhales.com
Excursions leave daily, May–October.

A Cape Ann Whale Watch has been in operation since 1979 and boasts the largest and fastest whale watch vessel in Massachusetts. Whale sightings are guaranteed and include naturalists from the Whale Conservation Institute.

You don't have to look far to find free live music playing around the North Shore in the summer:

Andover has free concerts in the park on Chestnut Street on Wednesday evenings.

Georgetown has free concerts at the Kiwanis Ice House Performing Arts Pavilion, American Legion Park, off Prospect Street on Sunday evenings in July and August.

Gloucester has live music at the Thursday afternoon farmers' market in the harbor loop and in Stage Fort Park on Sundays at 7PM at the gazebo overlooking Gloucester Harbor.

Hamilton-Wenham has free concerts in the gazebo in Patton Park every Sunday in the summer at 5PM. Kids can dance and run around on the playground. Pack a picnic for the whole family to enjoy.

Ipswich has a great summer concert series at Castle Hill on the Crane Estate. Bring a blanket and some food, and listen to music on the hill on Thursday nights from 7PM to 9PM. Gates open at 5PM. Admission is $25 per car. Don't forget the bug spray!

Lawrence has farmers' market concerts at Appleton Way, between Essex and Common streets on Wednesday afternoons at 1PM.

Marblehead has a summer jazz concerts series, with six to eight evening concerts per summer held in downtown Marblehead.

Manchester-by-the-Sea has a free summer concert series on Tuesday nights in Masconomo Park from 6PM to 8PM.

Methuen has a few free concerts each summer in Greycourt Park, behind city hall. All shows are from 7PM to 8:30PM, and rain dates are usually the day after a concert.

Newburyport offers an outdoor summer concert series downtown at Waterfront Park, behind the Firehouse Center for the Arts.

Rockport has free summer concerts on Sunday nights from 7PM to 8:30PM at the Back Beach Bandstand. Children of all ages are welcome, and popcorn and soda are available.

Salem has a Berklee College of Music free summer concert series spotlighting talented local musicians at Derby Square in downtown Salem from 5PM to 7PM on various weekend nights. (Visit www.berklee.edu/events for days and times of events.)

Topsfield offers concerts on the green downtown.

Capt. Bill & Sons Whale Watch

24 Harbor Loop, Gloucester
978-283-6995 | www.captbillandsons.com

Capt. Bill & Sons Whale Watch is a family-owned company. Whale sightings are guaranteed, and naturalists from the Whale Center of New England narrate all trips. Make your reservations online.

Essex River Cruises & Charters/Clambakes

35 Dodge Street, Essex
978-768-6981 | www.essexcruises.com

Cruise up the river to see historic homes, shipyards, islands, beaches, marshes, birds, and wildlife. The cruises are narrated and have bathrooms.

The Great Marsh

Batchelder's Landing, Rowley
978-462-9988 | www.greatmarsh.org

Take a tour of the largest salt marsh in New England, including more than twenty thousand acres of marsh, beach, tidal river, estuary, mudflats, and islands, which makes it a breathtaking place for hiking, boating, bird watching, or fishing. Boat tours leave from Batchelder's Landing; park at the Rowley Commuter Rail Station on Railroad Avenue in Rowley. Batchelder's Landing is a five-minute walk toward the river.

Harbor Tours

23 Harbor Loop, Gloucester
978-283-1979 | www.capeannharbortours.com

Nothing says coastal New England like a lighthouse tour. Take the kids on this two-hour tour of Gloucester Harbor and the Annisquam River to learn about the role lighthouses have played in seafaring history.

Seven Seas Whale Watch

Seven Seas Wharf, Rogers Street, Gloucester
888-283-1776 | www.7Seas-WhaleWatch.com

Take the kids to sea, and see a whale! Experienced naturalists bring the excursion to life!

Greater Newburyport

Plum Island Ecotours
Black Cow Restaurant, Newburyport
978-273-2060 | www.piecotours.com
Adults, $30; children, $15.

Take a two-and-a-half-hour cruise aboard the *Joppa Flats*, which travels through the Great Marsh within the Parker River National Wildlife Refuge. You're encouraged to bring binoculars, a camera, lunch, and weather gear. Call ahead for reservations and departure times as the tour is dependent upon the tides.

Greater Salem

Salem Ferry—Boston's Best Cruises
10 Blaney Street, Salem
617-770-0040 | www.bostonsbestcruises.com

Travel to downtown Boston by boat in less than an hour. On the way, you'll get a harbor tour of Marblehead, Salem, and Boston harbors, including five lighthouses. This is an adventurous way to get into the city for some exploring. When you're done, take the ferry back to downtown Salem. Ferries have concession bars, restrooms, and climate-controlled cabins. Make sure you ask about family packages and discounts at participating restaurants, shops, and attractions in Boston and Salem. Free parking in Salem.

Other Fun Outings

Cape Ann

Bearskin Neck
Bearskin Neck, Rockport
www.town.rockport.ma.us

There is nothing sweeter than a family stroll down Bearskin Neck. Stop at Tuck's Candy to see the saltwater taffy being made. Lunch at the Top Dog. (Try the Golden Retriever: a hot dog with mac and cheese on top!) Grab an ice cream cone at Molly's. Hit the Rockport Fudgery to see the fudge being made. (Try one of their delicious truffle chocolate chip cookies!) Enjoy the ocean views, people watching, and boutique shopping. When you get home, make sure everyone brushes his or her teeth!

Nights on the Neck
Rocky Neck, Gloucester
978-282-0917 | www.rockyneckartcolony.org/notn.html

Make sure your family gets its culture fix! From June to October, the Rocky Neck Art Colony celebrates Nights on the Neck on the first Thursday of every month from 5PM to 9PM. Many galleries host receptions with refreshments, musicians, dancers, and other entertainers.

The Paper House
52 Pigeon Hill Street, Rockport
978-546-2629 | www.paperhouserockport.com
Adults, $2.50; kids under 6, free.

Give the kids a lesson on the virtues of recycling when you visit this house made entirely of paper. Since the house is small, you'll want to have other activites planned in downtown Rockport to make the trip worthwhile.

Greater Salem

Kimball Farm Corn Maze
780 East Broadway, Haverhill
978-521-3990 | www.kimballfarmcornmaze.com

Kids will love to get lost—and found—in this twisting, turning corn maze.

North Shore Navigators Professional Baseball
Fraser Field, 365 Western Avenue, Lynn

781-595-9400 | www.nsnavs.com
Game tickets, $6; group rate, $4.25; full-season family five pack, $100.

Summer means baseball, but if you don't want to break the bank getting to Fenway, consider a North Shore Navigators game. The Navs are part of the New England Collegiate Baseball League. College athletes come from all over the country to compete in this family-friendly league.

Paradise Mini Golf
Just off Route 114, Danvers/Middleton
978-750-4653 | www.paradiseminigolf.com
Year-round; see website for specific hours.

Bring the family to play eighteen holes, featuring a thirty-five-foot-high tree house, waterfalls, rivers, and feed the fish in the koi pond. After your game, grab some delicious locally made ice cream.

Richardson's
156 South Main Street, Middleton
978-774-5450 | www.richardsonsicecream.com

Grab an ice cream cone and visit with the cows and baby calves. There are also batting cages and a mini golf course for older kids—go before noon for the best prices.

Salem Trolley
Visitor's Center, 2 New Liberty Street, Salem
978-744-5469 | www.salemtrolley.com

For a double dose of education and entertainment, take the kids on an old-fashioned narrated trolley tour through downtown Salem.

Salem Willows Park and Winter Island
Fort Avenue, Salem
978-745-0251 | www.salemwillowspark.com
Daily, from 10AM. Hours subject to change.

Salem Willows Park has an arcade with games like pinball, air hockey, and skeeball, plus kiddie rides like a carousel and the Himalaya Ride. Peppy's Pizza next door serves thin crust Italian pizza and is open daily, 10AM–11PM, and there's also an ice cream shop along the strip. Moms recommend packing your hand sanitizer, as the old carnival atmosphere may leave you feeling a little bit icky.

The Topsfield Fairgrounds
207 Boston Street, Topsfield
978-887-5000 | www.topsfieldfair.org

There's always something happening at the Topsfield Fairgrounds, including the farmers' market every Saturday, frequent horse shows, aviary shows, antique car shows, and apple picking. And of course, there is always *the* Topsfield Fair, held annually each fall.

Merrimack Valley

Jay Gee's Ice Cream and Fun Center
602 Lowell Street, Methuen
978-689-0456 | jaygees.com
Seasonal; see website for hours of operation.
Go-kart family track, $5; batting cages, $1.25 per twelve pitches;
mini golf, $5 per person and $4 for children five and under.

Here's some fun for the whole family: Jay Gee's has go-karts, batting cages, mini golf, bumper cars, and homemade ice cream! Double seat go-karts are available for children under the fifty-four-inch height requirements. Children must be at least three years old and ride with a licensed driver. Jay Gee's also hosts birthday parties. See the website for details.

Lowell Spinners
450 Aiken Street, Lowell (LeLacheur Park)
978-459-2255 | www.lowellspinners.com

This is a great, budget-friendly sports outing for your family right here on the North Shore. The Lowell Spinners are a minor league baseball team, with home games Monday through Friday at 7:05PM and Saturday and Sunday at 5:05PM. Arrive early to find free parking on the street and get player autographs. If you've got a little slugger at home, consider hosting a birthday party at a home game—see the website for details. Note: no outside food or drinks are allowed to be brought into LeLacheur Park.

MSPCA Animal Care and Adoption Center at Nevins Farm
400 Broadway, Methuen
978-687-7453 | www.mspca.org

This fifty-five-acre animal care complex has an amazing pet adoption center. There's a room filled with cats, a dog section, and sections for rabbits, guinea pigs, birds, etc. Even if you're not adopting, kids will love to go and look at the animals. There's also a farm with horses, sheep, and other outdoor animals.

Farmers' Markets

Cape Ann

Cape Ann Farmers' Market
Stage Fort Park, Gloucester
978-290-2717 | www.capeannfarmersmarket.org
End of June through beginning of October, Thursdays, 3PM–6:30PM.

The Cape Ann Farmers' Market attracts at least twelve hundred visitors per market, featuring music, work by local artists, educational booths, children's activities, cooking demonstrations, and—of course—plenty of fresh nutrient-rich, locally grown food.

Greater Newburyport

Ipswich Farmers' Market
EBSCO parking lot, 10 Estes Street, Ipswich
978-356-0449
Early July through mid-October, Saturdays, 9AM–1PM.

Newburyport Farmers' Market
Tannery Marketplace, 50 Water Street, Newburyport
978-457-6644 | www.thenewburyportfarmersmarket.org
May through October, Sundays, 9AM–1PM.

The Newburyport Farmers' Market operates rain or shine, featuring live performances, locally grown foods, goods from local artisans, and more.

Rowley Farmers' Market
Rowley Town Common, Route 1A, Rowley
978-948-7506
July through September, Sundays, 8AM–1PM.

West Newbury Farmers' Market
Grange Hall, 21 Garden Street, West Newbury
978-352-2986
July through October, Saturdays, 9AM–noon.

Greater Salem

Beverly Farmers' Market
Veteran's Park, Rantoul Street and Railroad Avenue, Beverly
978-473-9891 | www.beverlyfarmersmarket.org
End of June to October, Mondays, 3:30PM–6:45PM.

The Beverly Farmers' Market features live music, fresh locally grown food, cheeses, pies, breads, and more.

Lynn Farmers' Market
Exchange and Washington streets, Central Square, Lynn
781-346-6726
July through October, Thursdays, 11AM–3PM.

At the Lynn Farmers' Market, you'll find local produce, bread, flowers, and other goods from local vendors.

Marblehead Farmers' Market

Middle School on Vine Street, Marblehead
781-631-1243 | www.marbleheadfm.com
June through October, Saturdays, 9AM–noon.

The Marblehead Farmers' Market features live music, coffee, homemade food, tons of fresh vegetables, cheeses, samples, fresh pasta, pies, breads, and more.

Peabody Farmers' Market

Railroad Avenue, Peabody (next to the Little Depot Diner and behind the courthouse)
978-538-5770 | www.peabody-ma.gov
July through October, Tuesdays, 1PM–6PM.

Salem Farmers' Market

Derby Square, Front Street, Salem
978-744-0004, ext. 15 | www.salemfarmersmarket.org
Mid-June through mid-October, Thursdays, 3PM–7PM.

The Salem Farmers' Market is a community market for fresh fruits and veggies, fresh lobsters, hand-made soaps, and other goods. The market is held rain or shine and also features live music and cooking demonstrations.

Saugus Farmers' Market

Cliftondale Square, exit off of Route 1, Jackson Street
781-233-1855
July through October, Tuesdays, 10AM–3PM.

The Saugus Farmers' Market has fresh, locally grown produce, flowers, homemade foods, and more.

Topsfield Farmers' Market

Topsfield Fairgrounds, Route 1
978-922-1648
July through September, Saturdays, 7AM–noon.

Merrimack Valley

Andover Farmers' Market
97 Main Street, Andover
978-475-2236 | www.andoverhistorical.org/farmersmarket
End of June through early October, Saturdays, 12:30PM–3:30PM.

The Andover Farmers' Market features locally grown produce and homemade foods, local artisan products such as homemade soaps and candles, plus family-friendly activities such as face painting, crafts, games, and live music.

Haverhill Farmers' Market
40 Bailey Boulevard, Haverhill
978-373-4377 | www.haverhillfarmersmarket.com
Mid-July through October, Saturdays, 8AM–1PM.

The Haverhill Farmers' Market features fruits and vegetables, baked goods, music, and even free community yoga classes! Don't miss the fall Harvest Festival, complete with pony rides.

Lawrence Farmers' Market
Parking lot across from Greater Lawrence Family Health Center, 216 Lawrence Street, Lawrence
978-974-0770 | www.groundworklawrence.org/farmersmarket
July through October, Saturdays, 10AM–2PM.

Fresh, healthy, delicious local fruits, vegetables, baked goods, jams, jellies, art, crafts, and more!

Sweet Treats

Indulge your little one's sweet tooth with a trip to one of these favorite ice cream shops, candy shops, or bakeries:

Captain Dusty's Ice Cream
60 Beach Street, Manchester-by-the-Sea
978-526-1663 | www.captaindustys.com

Captain Dusty's is a hot spot on a summer day. Families love it because they can cool off after a day at Singing Beach or take their ice cream across the street to the playground at Masconomo Park. Captain Dusty's also has locations in Beverly Farms and Salem.

Down River Ice Cream
241 John Wise Avenue, Essex
978-768-0102 | www.downrivericecream.net
Spring and summer. Daily, 11AM–9PM.

Sit back in an Adirondack chair and enjoy the views of the Great Marsh while you eat your take-out ice cream.

Harbor Sweets
85 Leavitt Street, Salem
800-243-2115 | www.harborsweets.com

Take a tour of the Harbor Sweets chocolate factory on Tuesdays and Thursdays at 11AM. (The company recommends calling ahead first.) You can find plenty of treats for under $10, plus assortments and sugar-free chocolates to sample after your tour.

Rockin' Cupcakes

42 Bearskin Neck, Rockport
978-852-8282

Rockin' Cupcakes has over twenty flavors of homemade cupcakes, plus ice cream, smoothies, and iced coffee.

The Rockport Fudgery

Tuna Wharf Road, Rockport
888-383-4379 | www.rockportfudgery.com

Watch fudge masters hand-whip the fudge with wooden paddles. You can ask for free samples and ship fudge around the country. Try one of the Fudgery's delicious chocolate truffle cookies.

Also try:

- **Cherry Hill Farm, Danvers**
- **Goodies, Danvers**
- **Molly's, Rockport**
- **Stowaway Sweets, Marblehead**
- **Turtle Alley, Gloucester and Salem**
- **White Farms Ice Cream, Ipswich**

Got a little kid who loves to watch *anything* that moves? Looking for a fun, inexpensive way to spend an afternoon? Try these ideas:

- Spend an afternoon at the Plum Island Airport in Newburyport, the oldest private airfield in the United States—it's a great place to sit and watch the planes take off and land. Or, try the municipal airport in Lawrence, which has a grassy area where kids can run around while they watch the planes take off. There's also a diner there called Joe's Landing that serves great banana or M&M pancakes and grilled cheese.

- Take a ride around Newburyport ... in a pedicab! Kids and adults alike will love the fresh-air tour. Rides are free (drivers work for tips.)

- Take a ride on the Salem Ferry or the Salem Trolley.

- Hop on the MBTA—try a trip into Boston's North End for authentic Italian pizza and pastries.

- Don't miss Sail Gloucester's Tall Ships Festival every Fourth of July weekend. Sit on the rocks at Stage Fort Park in Gloucester to watch the ships sail by.

- Gran Prix of Gloucester holds a world-renowned cyclo-cross event in September in Stage Fort Park, where athletes from around the world compete in a mix of road racing, mountain biking, and obstacle course running. Registration for a free kids' race is usually held following the main event.

- Have lunch at the Beach Street Café in Manchester-by-the-Sea or at the Subway in Gloucester. Sit and watch the MBTA trains go by from most tables.

⬧7 Child Care and Schools

An overview of early childhood education on the North Shore

Child Care

MAKING THE DECISION to go back to work—or not—is never an easy one. Whether because you need to, or because you want to, you may eventually find yourself looking for someone to help take care of your baby while you work. There's a world of options out there for safe, reliable, loving child care. Your choices may range from having a grandparent babysit, to choosing a center-based environment, a family-based daycare setting, a nanny in your own home, or even an au pair. There are pros and cons to each situation, and it all comes down to what works best for your own family's needs. You'll want to weigh factors like cost, schedule, socialization options, safety concerns, and general gut feelings about your child's happiness in a given child care setting. And, you'll also want to consider your back-up options for when your child—or your child care provider—is sick or on vacation.

If at all possible, try to start researching your options in advance of your baby's arrival, or at least long before you will return to work. Here, you'll find a few options to help jump-start a child care search.

Who's Who in Child Care Resources

Child Care Aware
800-424-2246 | www.childcareaware.org

A program of the National Association of Child Care Resource & Referral Agencies (NACCRRA), Child Care Aware helps families learn more about the elements of high-quality childcare and how to locate programs in their communities.

Childcare.gov
www.childcare.gov

Childcare.gov is a comprehensive online resource designed to link parents, child care providers, researchers, policy makers, and the general public with federal government sponsored child care and early learning information and resources. See their Choosing Childcare Checklists, as well as information on child care tax credits.

Education.com
www.education.com

For a list of daycare centers and preschools in your local area, try Education.com's Schoolfinder tool. (Select Find a School and input your city or zip code.)

Sitter City
www.sittercity.com

Sittercity.com is a site geared toward matching parents with local babysitters and nannies.

⚜ Pumping Before Returning to Work

Tip: If you plan to continue breastfeeding when you return to work and don't want to use formula, you'll need to start stockpiling breast milk in your freezer well ahead of your first day of work. Aim to have at least a week's supply in your freezer, which could actually take several weeks to accumulate when you're also nursing your baby. Once you're at work, you'll be bringing home an entire day's worth of milk on a daily basis, so what's in your freezer can become an emergency back-up supply, or can be used on days when your baby drinks more than you've pumped.

Preschool and Beyond

Before you know it, your baby's going to be donning a backpack and heading off for the first day of school. Whether that first day is for a toddler program, preschool, or kindergarten, Massachusetts state law says that all children must attend school beginning in September of the calendar year in which they turn six years old (and they must be at least five years old by the time school starts).

Most preschools begin enrolling children who are age 2.9 (two years, nine months) by the start of the school year, though some require that children are three years old by the start of the school year. Since public schools are mandated to provide educational programs for children turning three who've been determined to have a disability that impacts their ability to access a preschool curriculum, you'll see many public integrated preschool programs, where kids with an IEP (individualized education program) attend for free, and typically developing peer students may pay a tuition to attend. (For the sake of this chapter, typically developing students will be referred to as peers.) The children with disabilities participate in all classroom activities, with modifications as needed, while the peers serve as same-age role models and learn about empathy and working together.

In this chapter, we don't seek to recommend or review preschools around the North Shore, as there are quite literally hundreds of excellent options. And often, a preschool that makes sense for one family makes little sense for another family, due to parents' work schedules, drop-off and pick-up times, levels of required parent involvement, proximity to home, and so on. Choices for preschool can range from programs in the public school systems to private schools to church programs to co-op programs, Montessori schools, Waldorf schools, and more.

When it's time for your child to start preschool, you'll want to visit several of the schools that you think will make sense for your family. Call ahead to schedule a day to visit the school, meet the teachers, and observe the classroom environment. Ask questions about the school's curriculum, discipline policies, overall educational philosophy, admissions process, and tuition. When it's time to apply, you'll need to have records of your child's most recent physical and immunizations, plus your doctor's signature that your child is able to participate in school and/or camp. Keep in mind that some preschools will have more applications than spaces available, so you may be put on an admissions waiting list. For this reason, it may make sense to apply to several schools to guarantee a spot for your child.

Of course, where you decide to send your child to preschool, and later elementary and high school, may depend largely on the town in which you live. In this chapter, we've provided an overview of all the North Shore school districts, including contact information, websites, grades served, and whether the district offers a choice program where children from neighboring districts may be able to attend school in a town other than the one in which they reside. We've also included some stats to show how the towns stack up in terms of graduation rates and test scores, per pupil expenditures, and average home values and property taxes (see *Appendix*).

Most towns host a kindergarten registration event during the spring or summer before your child will enter kindergarten, and then set up separate kindergarten screening days. Check your district's website for kindergarten registration and screening dates. To register your child, you'll generally need to bring in proof of residency (a utility bill, rental agreement, lease, etc., with your name and address) and an original copy of your child's birth certificate, plus emergency and doctor contact information, including proof of immunizations and other health history forms, such as your child's most recent physical information. Check with your school to see what's required before you go to register. All towns are required to offer free half-day kindergarten; while many towns offer full-day kindergarten, some districts require parents to pay for this extended-day option. Many schools also offer before- and after-school programs for working parents. See your district's website for details.

And finally, perhaps what's most unique about schools on the North Shore is the sheer number of prestigious private schools. In this chapter, we've included a sampling of some of the more well-known schools, as well as some other unique offerings on the North Shore.

Public School District Profiles

Amesbury

10 Congress Street
Amesbury, MA 01913
978-388-0507 | www.amesburyma.gov
Title I District; offers inter-district school choice
Grades served: Pre-K–12

The Amesbury School District has two elementary schools (Cashman Elementary and Amesbury Elementary), plus a special education school, a charter school, a middle school, and a high school. The Amesbury pre-K program enrolls children with and without special needs. There's a morning session (8:30AM–11:15AM) and an afternoon session (12:15PM–3PM) for preschoolers, from Monday through Thursday. The program is held at Cashman Elementary School and Amesbury Elementary School. Kindergarten registration and screening is conducted in April.

Andover

36 Bartlet Street
Andover, MA 01810
978-623-8501 | www.aps1.net
Title I District; does not offer choice; accepts METCO students
Grades served: Pre-K–12
Average tuition for preschool (for peers) is $4,165 per year for five days; $3,438 for four days; $3,015 for three days. (Note that there is no two-day program available.) There's a 10 percent discount for twins and a 15 percent discount for triplets. Average tuition for full-day kindergarten is $4,400.

The Andover School District has six elementary schools, three middle schools, and a high school, plus two special education schools. Andover is also well-known for its many prestigious private schools. The preschool is an inclusive, multi-sensory program that serves children with special needs and peer students. Peers attend school for two and a half hours, either in the morning or the afternoon. Children must be three years of age, and peers must be fully potty trained to start preschool. The kindergarten registration packet is available online, as well as applications for reduced-fee tuition.

Beverly

502 Cabot Street
Beverly, MA 01915
978-921-6100 | www.beverlyschools.org
Title I District; offers choice; accepts METCO students
Grades served: Pre-K–12
Full- and half-day kindergarten is available. Half-day programs are free of charge and available at each elementary school. Full-day kindergarten is $400 per month.

The Beverly School District has five elementary schools, a middle, and high school, plus several special education schools, including the Beverly School for the Deaf and the world-renowned Landmark School. There are also many options for private school in Beverly. Beverly offers various models of preschool education, including an integrated program, combining special-needs children with age appropriate peers; intensive preschool, designed for students with significant social and cognitive deficits; and related services for special education students who receive individual or small group therapy sessions. Preschool screenings are conducted each year for children ages three to five in September, January, and April. Kindergarten placement is done by a lottery system, and every effort is made to place all the children in half- and full-day programs at their neighborhood schools whenever possible.

Boxford

28 Middleton Road
Boxford, MA 01921
978-887-0771 | www.boxfordschools.org
Grades served: Pre-K–6
Three full-days of kindergarten are free; tuition is required for the other two days. Average tuition for kindergarten is $3,360. Preschool tuition ranges from $1,580 per year to $3,150 per year, depending on the program selected, with a 10 percent discount for siblings.

The Boxford elementary schools, part of the Tri-Town School Union, are the Harry Lee Cole (grades K–2) and Spofford Pond schools (grades 3–6). Harry Lee Cole offers an integrated preschool program designed to serve children with mild to moderate special needs and also includes three- and four-year-old peer students. Preschool options include morning or afternoon schedules for two, three, or four days. Lunch buddies and extended-day options are offered based on availability. Three or five full-day kindergarten is offered. Students continuing in the public school system will attend Masconomet Regional Schoool District, which serves Boxford, Middleton, and Topsfield.

Danvers
64 Cabot Road
Danvers, MA 01923
978-777-4539 | www.danvers.mec.edu
Title I District; does not offer choice; accepts METCO students
Grades served: Pre-K–12
Free, full-day kindergarten is offered in the district.

Danvers has five elementary schools, a middle school, and high school, plus a special education school and several private schools. Preschool is offered for special education students only, though some three- and four-year-olds may be chosen to be peer models in the preschool. Call student services at 978-774-6112 to see if your child may be eligible.

Essex
See *Manchester/Essex Regional School District.*

Georgetown
51 North Street
Georgetown, MA 01833
978-352-5777 | www.georgetown.k12.ma.us
Title I District; offers choice; accepts METCO students
Grades served: Pre-K–12
Preschool tuition ranges from $1,480 per year to $7,320 per year, depending on the program selected.

Georgetown has two public elementary schools, plus a middle and high school. The Perley Elementary School houses grades pre-K–1 and has an integrated preschool program designed to serve children with a wide range of disabilities as well as meet the needs of peer students. Half- and full-day sessions are offered for two-, three-, and five-day options. All students must participate in a screening program.

A Parent's Guide to Choosing Safe and Healthy Child Care

Tips and Guidelines

Here you'll find some fantastic tips produced by the National Resource Center for Health and Safety in Child Care for choosing a quality place for your child. You can copy what's here or go online and print out copies. I suggest printing a copy for every center you visit and taking notes during your visit or immediately after. This way you'll have a record of your impressions when you start to review your options.

Supervision
Are children supervised at all times, even when they are sleeping?

Hand Washing and Diapering
Do all caregivers and children wash their hands often, especially before and after eating, using the bathroom, and changing diapers?

Director Qualifications
Does the director of a child care center have a bachelor's degree in a child-related field?

Lead Teacher Qualifications
Does the lead teacher in a child care center have a bachelor's degree in a child-related field? Has the teacher worked in child care for at least one year?

Child Staff Ratio and Group Size
How many children are being cared for in the child care center? The younger the children are, the more caregivers there should be.

Immunizations
Does the child care program have records proving that all children in care are up-to-date on all their required immunizations?

Toxic Substances
Are toxic substances like cleaning supplies and pest killers kept away from children?

Emergency Plan
Does the child care program have an emergency plan if a child is injured, sick, or lost? Does the child care program have information about who to contact in an emergency?

Fire Drills
Does the child care program have a plan in case of a disaster like a fire, tornado, flood, blizzard, or earthquake?

Child Abuse
Can caregivers be seen by others at all times, so a child is never alone with one caregiver? Have all caregivers been trained how to prevent child abuse, how to recognize signs of child abuse, and how to report suspected child abuse?

Medications
Does the child care program keep medication out of reach from children?

Staff Training and First Aid
Have caregivers been trained how to keep children healthy and safe from injury and illness?

Playgrounds
Is the playground inspected often for safety? Are the soil and playground surfaces checked often for dangerous substances and hazards?

Gloucester

6 School House Road
Gloucester, MA 01930
978-281-9800 | www.gloucester.k12.ma.us
Title I District; offers choice; accepts METCO students
Grades served: Pre-K–12
Free, full-day kindergarten. Peer tuition for the integrated public preschool program is $50 per week.

The Gloucester Public School District has five elementary schools, a middle, and a high school. Gloucester offers an integrated public preschool program with limited spaces for peers. To register, call 978-281-9848 in March to make an appointment for registration and screening. Children on individual education plans are free and peers pay a tuition. Morning sessions are from 8:30AM to 10:50AM, and afternoon sessions run from 12:05PM to 2:30PM. There's also an extended-day lunch hour option for an extra cost of $20 per week. Gloucester collaborates with Head Start to help families who cannot afford tuition.

Groveland (Pentucket Regional School District)

253 School Street
Groveland, MA 01834
978-372-8856 | www.prsd.org
Non-Title I School
Grades served: Pre-K–12

The Pentucket Regional School District comprises the three towns of Merrimac, Groveland, and West Newbury. The district's schools include four elementary schools (grades pre-K–6), a middle school (grades 7 and 8), and a senior high school (grades 9–12). The district offers integrated preschool programs at the Dr. Elmer S. Bagnall School in Groveland, the Dr. John C. Page School in West Newbury, and the Dr. Frederick N. Sweetsir School in Merrimac. Kindergarten is offered at all four elementary schools—screening and registration are required. See the website for details.

Hamilton (Hamilton-Wenham Regional School District)
5 School Street
Wenham, MA 01984
978-468-5310 | www.hwschools.net
Title I District; offers choice; accepts METCO students
Grades served: Pre-K–12
Free half-day kindergarten; full-day kindergarten is $4,000 per year.

The Hamilton-Wenham Regional School District has three elementary schools, a middle, and high school. The preschool is an integrated program with 50 percent special education and 50 percent peer students. To enter into the program, children must participate in a screening and be selected. The peers chosen are charged a fee, and children on an IEP (individualized education plan) are free.

Haverhill
4 Summer Street
Haverhill, MA 01830
978-374-3405 | www.haverhill-ps.org
Title I District; offers choice; accepts METCO students
Grades served: Pre-K–12
Full-day kindergarten is $4,100 for Massachusetts residents. Half-day options are also available for free, in morning and afternoon sessions. A preschool program is offered at the Moody Preschool. Extended-daycare options are also available.

The Haverhill Public School District consists of a preschool, seven elementary schools, four middle schools, a high school, and two charter schools. The Moody Integrated Preschool is free for children on an IEP (individualized education plan) and offers services for students with challenges from severe autism to multiple handicaps. Peer students pay a tuition of $80 per week on a sliding scale, based on income. The program is four days per week, Monday through Thursday. A morning session is available from 9AM to 11:30AM, and an afternoon session meets from 12:45PM to 3:15PM. Half-day kindergarten is free in the Haverhill School District, with a morning and an afternoon session available. Parents can elect to pay for full-day kindergarten and extended-care options. Kindergarten registration is by appointment only. Call 978-420-1912 for more information. (Moody Preschool students do not need to register for kindergarten, but are automatically enrolled.)

Ipswich

1 Lord Square
Ipswich, MA 01938
978-356-2935 | www.ipswichschools.org
Title I District; offers choice; accepts METCO students
Grades served: Pre-K–12
Integrated preschool has morning and afternoon sessions; $2,000 per year tuition is based on four days per week. Free full-day kindergarten.

The Ipswich public schools consist of two elementary schools, a middle, and high school, plus a special education school. Ipswich offers enrichment programs for academically gifted students at the elementary schools. The Ipswich integrated preschool program combines special-needs and peer children together in a positive environment that respects the individual development of all children and allows them to learn at their own pace. To enroll in the Ipswich preschool programs, a child must first complete a developmental screening, offered each spring to the community, and by appointment, when necessary. There are a limited number of openings, so apply early.

Lawrence

255 Essex Street
Lawrence, MA 01840
978-975-5900 | www.lawrence.k12.ma.us
Title I District; does not offer choice; accepts METCO students
Grades served: Pre-K–12
Free full-day kindergarten.

The Lawrence Public School District comprises four early childhood centers, ten elementary schools, six middle schools, eight high schools, and two charter schools. Pre-K programs are offered at three of the elementary schools: the James F. Hennessey School, the John Breen School, and the John R. Rollins School. Full-day kindergarten is offered at each of these schools and also at the James I. Lawlor School. Lawrence offers an integrated preschool program, with half-day morning or afternoon sessions five days per week. The approximately one hundred seventy-five seats available in preschool fill up fairly quickly, so if you are a Lawrence resident and are interested in this program, you need to contact the early childhood center closest to you to arrange for a preschool screening. Screenings are held

The National Association for the Education of Young Children (NAEYC), founded in 1926, has nearly ninety thousand members worldwide. Here's some advice from them; much more can be found on their website (www.naeyc.org), including a database of schools accredited by them.

1. A good program will provide parents an opportunity to visit, stay a while, and get a good sense of the environment.

2. Parents should ask about and observe group sizes and the number of teaching staff in each classroom. For preschoolers, group size should not exceed twenty children with at least two teaching staff always present.

3. Play, including dramatic play and blocks and active play outdoors, should be integrated into classroom topics of study. Play not only supports children's intellectual development, it is also very important for their physical development.

4. Programs should promote the health and nutrition of children.

5. Children in the program should be engaged with one another and their teachers. Listen and watch for a happy buzz of activity—neither too quiet nor too loud.

6. Teachers should use positive speech and be loving and responsive to a child.

7. A good program should be able to adapt to the needs of each individual child without ignoring the whole group.

8. A high-quality program should have strategies in place to attract and maintain a consistently qualified, well-trained staff and reduce staff turnover.

9. Programs should have a strong connection with the families of each child and the community as well.

10. Check that the program is licensed by the state.

Reprinted with permission by NAEYC.

the second Wednesday of each month. If your child does get a seat in the program, there is no cost for the preschool program. Sites of the early childhood centers are as follows:

Breen School
114 Osgood Street (South Lawrence) | 978-975-5932

Hennessey School
122 Hancock Street (Tower Hill) | 978-975-5950

Rollins School
451 Howard Street (Prospect Hill) | 978-722-8190

Parents can also contact the Early Childhood Education Department at 978-975-5905, ext. 25744.

Lynn
90 Commercial Street
Lynn, MA 01905
781-593-1680 | www.lynnschools.org
Title I District; does not offer choice; accepts METCO students
Morning and afternoon preschool sessions are offered at various schools, on a limited basis. Full-day kindergarten is free and located in all of the elementary schools.

The Lynn public schools have nine integrated preschool classrooms, and one Title I classroom (children who are four years old by September 1 are eligible for this program), located in various schools. Literacy rich classrooms provide opportunities for children to explore, make choices, and discover so that each child's unique capabilities flourish. Class sizes depend on the needs of the children served. Preschool screening is required and is offered in April to three- and four-year-old children who reside in Lynn and have been selected through a lottery. At the end of March each year, the Lynn Public Schools hosts an Education Fair where parents of three- and four-year-old children can complete and submit a form for the lottery. In order to be eligible for the lottery, a parent must fill out the form at the Education Fair. Kindergarten registration begins in March and is by appointment. (Call the Parent Information Center in February to schedule an appointment: 781-593-8796, ext. 3175.)

Lynnfield

55 Summer Street
Lynnfield, MA 01940
781-334-9200 | www.lynnfield.k12.ma.us
Title I District; does not offer choice; accepts METCO students
Grades served: Pre-K–12

Morning and afternoon preschool sessions are available. Tuition is $2,000 per year for two days; $3,000 per year for three days; $4,000 per year for four days; $5,000 per year for five days. Half-day kindergarten is free, and parents can opt for full-day kindergarten for $2,600 per year.

Lynnfield has a preschool, two elementary schools, a middle school, and a high school. Lynnfield Preschool offers morning and afternoon sessions. The morning program has two-, three-, and five-day classes available. The afternoon program has two-, three-, and four-day classes. To register your child, stop by your local elementary school to speak with the secretary and to get orientation dates. Or, call the Special Services Office at 781-581-5140.

Manchester/Essex

36 Lincoln Street, PO Box 1407
Manchester, MA 01944
978-526-4919 | www.mersd.org
Title I District; offers choice; accepts METCO students
Grades served: Pre-K–12

Morning integrated preschool offered. Kindergarten is free, full day, with a half day on Wednesdays. (First month is all half days.)

The Manchester/Essex Regional School District has two elementary schools, a middle school, and a high school. Manchester also has the world-renowned Landmark School for special education, as well as many good options for private schools. The Manchester Essex Integrated Preschool has two sessions: Monday/Wednesday/Friday and Tuesday/Thursday. The programs run from 8:30AM to noon each day. Peer Pal applications may be taken throughout the school year for the following fall class. Peer Pals need to be 2.9 by August 31 to be admitted for that school year. Peer Pal slots are determined after students receiving special services are placed. Contact the Special Education Office for additional information: 978-768-1192.

Marblehead

9 Widger Road
Marblehead, MA 01945
781-639-3141 | www.marbleheadschools.org
Title I District; does not offer choice; accepts METCO students
Grades served: Pre-K–12
Tuition for full-day kindergarten is $2,547 annually.

The Marblehead public school system consists of five elementary schools, a middle, and high school, plus a charter school and a special education school. An integrated pre-K program is held at the Bell School.

Merrimac (Pentucket Regional School District)

104 Church Street
Merrimac, MA 01860
978-346-8319 | www.prsd.org
Title I School
Grades served: Pre-K–12
Full-day kindergarten is $3,500 per year.

The Pentucket Regional School District comprises the three towns of Merrimac, Groveland, and West Newbury. The district's schools include four elementary schools (grades pre-K–6), a middle school (grades 7 and 8), and a senior high school (grades 9–12). The district offers integrated preschool programs at the Dr. Elmer S. Bagnall School in Groveland, the Dr. John C. Page School in West Newbury, and the Dr. Frederick N. Sweetsir School in Merrimac. Kindergarten is offered at all four elementary schools—screening and registration are required. See the website for details.

How the Towns Stack Up

See the *Appendix* for information on graduation rates for four-year high schools, per pupil expenditures by district, SAT reports, average property taxes, and average price of single family homes around the North Shore.

Methuen

90 Hampshire Street
Methuen, MA 01844
978-722-6001 | www.methuen.k12.ma.us
Title I District; does not offer choice; accepts METCO students
Grades served: Pre-K–12
Preschool tuition ranges from $11 per day to $18 per day, depending on family income. Half-day kindergarten is offered with a full-day option for $3,200 per year.

The Methuen Public School District provides an integrated preschool program that includes spaces for peer role models. (Students are assigned to home schools if possible.) Children must be three years old by September. Methuen's Rangerland Preschool offers a two-and-a-half-hour program three days a week for children who are ages four to five by September. Classes meet from 9AM to 11:30AM, Monday, Tuesday, and Wednesday, with an occasional Thursday. Spaces are limited to sixteen children. Preschool applications for peer role models in Methuen integrated preschool classes are typically available at all grammar schools in early March. For further information about the preschool, please call 978-722-6040, ext. 2386.

Middleton

28 Middleton Road
Boxford, MA 01921
978-887-0771 | www.tritownschoolunion.com
Title I District; does not offer choice; accepts METCO students
Grades served: Pre-K–6
Two full days and a half day of kindergarten are offered for free.

The Tri-Town School Union serves the elementary schools of Boxford, Middleton, and Topsfield. Middleton public schools' integrated preschool language-based classes were established in 1990 for peers as well as those with special needs. If you have questions regarding the program, you can contact the preschool coordinator at 978-750-4756, ext. 614. The kindergarten program in Middleton is the two-and-a-half-day model. Children attend either Monday morning and Wednesday and Friday all day, or Monday afternoon and Tuesday and Thursday all day. Enrollment is based upon geographical location within town. Students go on to the Masconomet Regional School District middle and high school.

Nahant

290 Castle Road
Nahant, MA 01908
781-581-1600 | www.johnsonschool.org
Title I District; does not offer choice
Grades served: Pre-K–6
Five-day preschool program is $4,600; three-day is $2,760; two-day is $1,840.

Nahant has one elementary school, a middle school, and a high school. Nahant has an integrated preschool program at the Johnson Elementary School, with theme-based education on topics such as dinosaurs, plants, and the ocean.

Newbury (Triton Regional School District)

Newbury Elementary Public School
112 Elm Street
Byfield, MA 01922
978-465-2397 | www.trsd.net
Title I District; offers choice; accepts METCO students
Tuition for preschool program of two half days is $1,550 per year; three half days, $2,100 per year; four half days, $2,500 per year.

The Triton Regional School District, which serves the towns of Newbury, Rowley, and Salisbury, has three elementary schools, a middle school, and a high school. The district's preschool programs are half-day classes at Newbury Elementary School, Pine Grove School, and Salisbury Elementary School for two or three mornings or afternoons a week, or four afternoons a week. All inclusive classrooms serve special-needs and peer students. While tuition is charged, there is financial assistance available. Open house and preliminary registration occur in April, and spaces are limited.

There are two options for kindergarten in the district: a traditional half-day program (morning or afternoon) or a tuition-based full-day program. Depending upon enrollment, there may be a lottery for slots in the full-day kindergarten program. An information night is held in late winter, and registration and screening take place in early May. Bus transportation is provided for all children attending kindergarten. Children must be three years of age by August 31 to register for preschool and five years of age for kindergarten.

Newburyport

70 Low Street
Newburyport, MA 01950
978-465-4457 | www.newburyport.k12.ma.us
Title I District; offers choice; accepts METCO students
Grades served: Pre-K–12
Preschool, plus full-day and half-day kindergarten are offered. Pre-K tuition is $200 per month for two days; $245 per month for three days; $290 per month for four days; $335 per month for five days. Tuition for full-day kindergarten for 2010–2011 was $3,500.

The Newburyport Public School District has three elementary schools, a middle school, and a high school, plus a charter school and several options for private schools. Pre-K is offered from 8:45AM to 3:15PM. (Half-day pre-K is offered in the morning from 8:45AM to 11:15AM or in the afternoon from 12:45PM to 3:15PM.) Kindergarten runs from 9AM to 3:30PM. (Half-day kindergarten is offered in the morning from 9AM to 11:30AM or in the afternoon from 1PM to 3:30PM.)

North Andover

1600 Osgood Street
Suite 3-59
North Andover, MA 01845
978-794-1503 | www.northandoverpublicschools.com
Title I District; does not offer choice; accepts METCO students
Grades served: Pre-K–12
Full- and half-day kindergarten is offered. Preschool tuition is $280 per month or $2,800 per year. Tuition for full-day kindergarten is on a sliding fee scale, with an average tuition of $2,700 per year.

The North Andover School District has five elementary schools, a middle school, a high school, plus a preschool. The area is also known for its prestigious private schools. The preschool CUBS program (children united by special abilities) and the Atkinson School kindergarten programs are housed at a new early childhood center located at 115 Phillips Brooks

Road. Morning and afternoon sessions are available for preschool (two and a half hours, Monday through Thursday). All children are enrolled for the four days. Spaces are limited. Applications can be downloaded directly from the website. Kindergarten registration is required for all full- or half-day students, and screenings usually take place in the spring. Children must be five years of age by August 31 to be eligible for kindergarten and three years of age for preschool.

Peabody

21 Johnson Street
Peabody, MA 01960
978-536-6500 | www.peabody.k12.ma.us
Title I District; does not offer choice; accepts METCO students
Grades served: Pre-K–12
Free full-day kindergarten. Preschool tuition for children who do not qualify for special education is $3,600 per year.

The Peabody school system is made up of eight elementary schools, a middle school, and a high school. The Peabody integrated preschool program offers morning (8:45AM to 11:15AM) and afternoon (noon to 2:30PM) sessions. On Fridays, there's an alternating schedule for sessions off in order for teachers to engage in team meetings and program development. The classroom for children with Autism Spectrum Disorder is a full-day program, Monday through Thursday, from 8:35AM to 2:30PM. Kindergarten in the district is a free full-day program.

Rockport

24 Jerden's Lane c/o Rockport Public Schools
Rockport, MA 01966
978-546-1200 | www.rockport.k12.ma.us
Title I District; offers choice
Grades served: Pre-K–12
Tuition for preschool peers is $4,950 per year. Kindergarten in the district is a free full-day program.

The Rockport School District is a small district, with one elementary school, a middle school, and a high school, all on the same campus. Rockport Elementary has an integrated preschool program with a limited number of spaces for peers. Parents of peer students who would like to enroll their children in the program should call the school in March to set up a screening appointment, which usually takes place in April.

Rowley (Triton Regional School District)

Solstice School (Special Education School)
20 Bowlery Drive
Rowley, MA 01969
978-948-2346 | www.trsd.net
Special Education Approved: Yes

Pine Grove (Public School)
191 Main Street
Rowley, MA 01969
978-948-2520 | www.trsd.net/pinegrove
Title I District; offers choice; accepts METCO students
Tuition for preschool program of two half days is $1,550 per year; three half days, $2,100 per year; four half days, $2,500 per year.

The Triton Regional School District, which serves the towns of Newbury, Rowley, and Salisbury, has three elementary schools, a middle school, and a high school. The district's preschool programs are half-day classes at Newbury Elementary School, Pine Grove School, and Salisbury Elementary School for two or three mornings or afternoons a week, or four afternoons a week. All inclusive classrooms serve special-needs children and peer children. While tuition is charged, there is financial assistance available. Open house and preliminary registration occur in April, and spaces are limited.

There are two options for kindergarten in the district: a traditional half-day program (morning or afternoon) or a tuition-based full-day program. Depending upon enrollment, there may be a lottery for slots in the full-day kindergarten program. An information night is held in late winter, and registration and screening take place in early May. Bus transportation is provided for all children attending kindergarten. Children must be three years of age by August 31 to register for preschool and five years of age for kindergarten.

Salem

29 Highland Avenue
Salem, MA 01970
978-740-1212 | salemk12.org
Title I District; does not offer choice; accepts METCO students

Grades served: Pre-K–12
Preschool is $70 per week. Free full-day kindergarten.

The Salem Public School District consists of six elementary schools, a middle school, a high school, a charter school, and the Horace Mann Laboratory School. The Salem Early Childhood Center offers two preschool sessions a day. Sessions are two and a half hours a day, Monday through Thursday. The morning session is from 8:30AM to 11AM; afternoons are noon to 2:30PM. Classes are integrated, where students with special needs and peer students are educated together. In addition, there are at-risk classrooms where students who may be at risk educationally receive high-quality instruction. Three special-needs kindergarten classrooms are part of the Early Childhood Center. These classes follow the regular Bentley Elementary School year dates and hours.

Salisbury (Triton Regional School District)

Salisbury Elementary
100 Lafayette Road
Salisbury, MA 01952
978-463-5852 | www.trsd.net/salisbury
Title I District; offers choice; accepts METCO students
Tuition for preschool program of two half days is $1,550 per year; three half days, $2,100 per year; four half days, $2,500 per year.

The Triton Regional School District, which serves the towns of Newbury, Rowley, and Salisbury, has three elementary schools, a middle school, and a high school. The district's preschool programs are half-day classes at Newbury Elementary School, Pine Grove Elementary School, and Salisbury Elementary School for two or three mornings or afternoons a week, or four afternoons a week. All inclusive classrooms serve special-needs children and peer children. While tuition is charged, there is financial assistance available. Open house and preliminary registration occur in April, and spaces are limited.

There are two options for kindergarten in the district: a traditional half-day program (morning or afternoon) or a tuition-based full-day program. Depending upon enrollment, there may be a lottery for slots in the full-day kindergarten program. An information night is held in late winter, and registration and screening take place in early May.

Bus transportation is provided for all children attending kindergarten. Children must be three years of age by August 31 to register for preschool and five years of age for kindergarten.

Saugus

23 Main Street
Saugus, MA 01906
781-231-5000 | www.saugus.k12.ma.us
Title I District; does not offer choice
Grades served: Pre-K–12
Full-day pre-K is $4,200 per year. Morning session only is $2,200 per year; afternoon session is $1,800 per year. Full-day kindergarten is $1,960.

The Saugus Public School District consists of four elementary schools, an early childhood center, a middle school, and a high school. Preschool is held at the Early Childhood Center at the Ballard School. Parents should call the school in early April to schedule a screening appointment (781-231-5000, ext. 108). Enrollment in the pre-K program is on a first come, first served basis. A $100 deposit is required to reserve a space. Full-day, morning, and afternoon sessions are available. Full-day kindergarten is available for a fee, with a $100 deposit required.

Swampscott

207 Forest Avenue
Swampscott, MA 01907
781-596-8800 | www.swampscott.k12.ma.us
Title I District; does not offer choice; accepts METCO students
Grades served: Pre-K–12
Pre-K tuition for five days is $260 per month; three days, $150 per month; two days, $100 per month. Half-day kindergarten is free; extended day for a fee.

The Swampscott School District has three elementary schools, a middle school, and a high school. The Swampscott Integrated Preschool offers two-, three-, and five-day programs. Registration for preschool begins in January, and screening is required. Students who are currently enrolled in the program and siblings of students in the program have first preference for available placements. Children must be three years of age to receive services or enroll in the integrated preschool program. Speech therapy, occupational therapy, physical therapy, and vision therapy occur in the program weekly. Kindergarten registration begins in February. Half-day kindergarten runs from 8:30AM to noon. A registration packet will be sent home stating the requirements for enrollment. Children must be five years old by September 1 to be eligible for kindergarten.

Topsfield (Masconomet Regional School District)

20 Endicott Road
Topsfield, MA 01983
978-887-2323 | www.masconomet.org
Title I District; does not offer choice
Grades served: Pre-K–12

Average preschool tuition rates for two days is $151 per month; three days, $222 per month; four days, $297 per month; five days, $345 per month. Extended-day options are also available. Kindergarten is free for three full days; tuition is charged for the other two days.

The Masconomet Regional School District serves the towns of Boxford, Middleton, and Topsfield, consisting of two elementary schools, a middle school, and a high school. The Steward Elementary School serves children in pre-K to grade 3. Tuition-based preschool is available for two-, three-, four-, or five-day sessions. The full-day kindergarten has two sessions: Session A is Monday, Wednesday, and Thursday from 8:45AM to 3:10PM. Session B is Tuesday, Wednesday, and Friday from 8:45AM to 3:10PM. An optional tuition-based five full-day program is also available.

Wenham (Hamilton-Wenham Regional School District)

See *Hamilton.*

West Newbury (Pentucket Regional School District)

See *Groveland.*

For a list of preschools in your city, check out Savvy Source's Massachusetts page: www.savvysource.com.

A Sampling of Some of the Area's Unique Offerings

Cape Ann

Cape Ann Waldorf School
701 Cabot Street, Beverly
978-927-8811 | www.capeannwaldorf.org
Grades: K–8
Average annual tuition is $4,230 for two-day nursery; $6,320 for three-day nursery; $9,970 for five-day nursery; $8,530 for four-day kindergarten; $9,970 for five-day kindergarten; $16,040 for grades 1 and 2; $17,700 for grades 3–8.

The Cape Ann Waldorf School is a K–8 school with an early childhood program that serves families with children from infancy through kindergarten age. The early childhood program emphasizes imaginative play, language development, artistic development, social skills, singing, storytelling, and movement. Children in the nursery and kindergarten programs learn about the world around them through activities such as baking bread, playing with puppets, and building with natural materials.

Eastern Point Day School
8 Farrington Avenue, Gloucester
978-283-1700 | www.easternpointdayschool.org
Grades: Pre-K–8
Average annual tuition for K–8 is $8,500, plus additional fees.

Eastern Point offers pre-K through grade 8 classes in a beautiful setting overlooking the ocean. The school boasts small class sizes, individualized curriculum, enrichment programs, and after-school programs. Families interested in Eastern Point Day School apply to the school during the academic year prior to the fall their child would enter.

St. Ann School

60 Prospect Street, Gloucester
978-283-3455 | www.stannsschool.com
Grades: Pre-K–8
Average annual tuition for K–8 is $3,850.

St. Ann School is a Catholic parochial school for grades pre-K to grade 8. Founded in 1885, the school has been educating children on Cape Ann for more than six generations. It is the only Catholic elementary school on Cape Ann.

Greater Newburyport

Immaculate Conception School (ICS)

1 Washington Street, Newburyport
978-465-7780 | www.icsnewburyport.com
Call for information about average tuition rates.

ICS is a coeducational Catholic school serving approximately three hundred students in pre-K through grade 8 from fifteen surrounding communities in Massachusetts and New Hampshire. In kindergarten, there are fifteen to sixteen students per class. Grades 1–8 average twenty-five to thirty students per class.

Inn Street Montessori School

52 Inn Street, Newburyport
978-463-0761 | www.innstreet.org
Grades: Pre-K–8
Average annual tuition is $10,400.

The Inn Street Montessori School is located in the heart of downtown Newburyport and offers lower elementary, upper elementary, and middle school classes serving children ages six to fourteen years of age.

Sparhawk School

259 Elm Street, Amesbury
978-388-5354 | www.sparhawkschool.com
Grades: K–8 to K-12
Average annual tuition is $1,300 per month for pre-K and kindergarten; upper elementary is $13,500 per year; grades 6–8, $14,600 per year.

Sparkhawk School is a private school serving students from pre-K to grade 12. The school was founded in 1994, with a philosophy of respect for children and trust in their inherent enthusiasm for learning.

Greater Salem

Brookwood School

1 Brookwood Road, Manchester-by-the-Sea
978-526-4500 | www.brookwood.edu
Grades: Pre-K–8
Average annual tuition begins at $16,040 for pre-K; pre-k extended day, add $3,360; K-8 ranges from $21,710–$27,155.

Founded in 1956, Brookwood School is a non-denominational coed day school for grades pre-K through 8. The school sits on thirty wooded acres on Boston's North Shore and enrolls approximately four hundred students, with a student to teacher ratio of 8:1. Brookwood offers the traditional academic areas of focus and a strong creative arts program.

The Clark School

487 Locust Street, Danvers
978-777-4699 | www.clarkschool.com
Grades: K–12
Average annual tuition for kindergarten to high school is $11,950.

The Clark School offers a multi-age learning environment for children in kindergarten through high school. Class sizes do not exceed fifteen students. The school emphasizes positive personal values, high achievement, and meaningful participation in the community.

Glen Urquhart School

74 Hart Street, Beverly
978-927-1064 | www.gus.org
Grades: K–8
Average annual tuition for kindergarten is $14,475; grades 6–8, $ 21,650.

Glen Urquhart is a coed independent day school for grades kindergarten through 8. The school serves 235 students from twenty-five towns and cities on the North Shore of Boston. This unique school was built on land once home to one of the largest, most famous, and most diverse orchid collections in the country. The school has incorporated the greenhouse space into classroom space, erasing boundaries between inside and out. The school offers a bright, sunny, colorful environment in which kids are encouraged to explore their intellects and develop their imaginations.

Harborlight Montessori School

243 Essex Street, Beverly
978-922-1008 | www.harborlightmontessori.org
Grades: Pre-K–8
Average annual tuition ranges from $7,500 for the two-day toddler program up to $15,050 for elementary and middle school.

Harborlight is an independent, coed day school. The school offers a cooperative learning community where students and adults not only honor but protect individualism. The Montessori classrooms are designed to be uncluttered, self-contained environments that encourage investigation and creativity, with hands-on learning materials.

Landmark School

429 Hale Street, PO Box 227, Prides Crossing
978-236-3010 | www.landmarkschool.org
Grades: 2–12
Average annual tuition is $45,000 for day students; $59,900 for residential students.

Landmark is a coed day and boarding school for children with learning disabilities. The school's mission is to enable and empower students with language-based learning disabilities to realize their educational and social potential through an exemplary school program complemented by outreach and training, diagnosis, and research. The school has a 1:3 teacher to student ratio and focuses on one-on-one learning.

Phoenix School
89 Margin Street, Salem
978-741-0870 | www.phoenixschool.org
Grades: K–8
Average annual tuition ranges from $15,500 for pre-K to grade 2, up to $16,600 for grades 5–8, with a 40 percent tuition discount for siblings.

Phoenix School is a coed day school located in the heart of the city of Salem. The school is committed to making use of community resources and being a vibrant part of the neighborhood, teaching students to accept responsibility for their lives in today's and tomorrow's world and to assume effective roles within their families and communities.

Shore Country Day School
545 Cabot Street, Beverly
978-927-1700 | www.shoreschool.org
Grades: Pre-K–9
Average annual tuition ranges from $21,070 for Readiness (pre-K) through grade 4; $28,900 for Grade 9.

Shore Country Day School is a coed day school that focuses on small classes, innovative teaching styles, and family partnerships. The school serves 435 boys and girls in grades Readiness (pre-kindergarten) through grade 9 and has a student to faculty ratio of 8:1.

Stoneridge Children's Montessori School
290 Hale Street, Beverly
978-927-0700 | www.stoneridgecms.org
Grades: Pre-K–8
Average annual tuition ranges from $8,650 for the three-day toddler program to $20,950 for middle school.

Stoneridge Children's Montessori School is an independent, coeducational

Montessori day school serving approximately 170 students in grades toddler (twenty-one months) through 8. The nine-and-a-half-acre campus serves twenty-six different communities around the North Shore. The school is founded on the Montessori vision of peace through education.

Tower School
75 West Shore Drive, Marblehead
781-631-5800 | www.towerschool.org
Grades: Pre-K–8
Average annual tuition ranges from $17,000 for pre-K to $23,750 for grades 6–8.

Tower School is an independent, coed day school for grades pre-K through 8. Founded in 1912, Tower is the oldest independent elementary school on Boston's North Shore. The school enrolls approximately three hundred students, with small classes being a hallmark of the school.

Merrimack Valley

Andover School of Montessori (ASM)
400 S Main Street, Andover
978-475-2299 | www.andomon.org
Grades: Pre-K–8
Average annual tuition ranges from $8,374 in pre-school to $14,209 for middle school.

Andover School of Montessori is a coed day school serving approximately two hundred students in four Children's House classrooms, three lower elementary, two upper elementary classrooms, and one middle school classroom. The school's vision is that ASM students will be learners for life: confident, independent, and always striving to enrich their lives by learning.

The Pike School

34 Sunset Rock Road, Andover
978-475-1197 | www.pikeschool.org
Grades: Pre-K–9
Average annual tuition ranges from $13,450 for pre-K to $27,260 for grade 9.

The Pike School is an independent, coeducational day school located on thirty-five woodland acres in Andover, Massachusetts. The school is committed to small class size and individual attention. The school enrolls about 430 students from thirty communities in northeastern Massachusetts and southern New Hampshire. Average class sizes are twelve in the lower school, up to fifteen in the upper school.

8 Enriching Adventures in Boston
Great ways to take advantage of all that Boston offers

IT WOULD BE a crime not to introduce your child to all the amazing art, culture, and history Boston has to offer—and if you think a two-year-old can't enjoy the opera, think again! Almost all of the city's theaters and orchestras offer family shows, sometimes even with children performing. Libraries are probably the richest resource around for free family fun—from story hours to puppet shows to author readings to free movies. All these events are catered to children, proving that the city really is their oyster.

As for museums, don't limit yourself to just the Children's Museum and the Museum of Science (though you certainly shouldn't miss them). Most of the museums in Boston have special programs for families, or at the very least, a few child-friendly exhibits that will keep them occupied long enough for parents and caregivers to get a well-deserved dose of grown-up culture. Try the Museum of Fine Arts treasure hunt; the materials the museum provides are perfectly geared to help you and your child navigate such a large museum. No matter what you choose, a day trip to the city allows you to expose your little one to some of the richest history in the United States—and a great deal of that history is readily accessible to the youngest set.

In addition to venue descriptions, you'll find age recommendations—but, again, take these for what they are worth. A mature toddler may enjoy the MIT Museum while a rambunctious five-year-old might find it a total bore; you know your child best. We've also tried to include membership information whenever possible, as this is a great way to save money. The overall benefit of having a yearly membership is that you'll be less attached to getting your money's worth out of one visit. Ancillary benefits, such as discounted parking, reciprocity with other museums or zoos, or priority tickets might also appeal to you. Either way, when you're not worrying about wasting money, everyone will have a much better time. Later, you and your kids will remember these excursions as wonderful urban adventures when you discovered the city together!

Libraries

Boston Public Central Library
700 Boylston Street, Boston
617-536-5400 | www.bpl.org
Monday–Thursday, 9AM–9PM; Friday–Saturday, 9AM–5PM; Sundays, 1PM-5PM.
Free.

A Founded in 1848 and opened in 1854, the main branch is the grand-daddy of Boston's libraries and was the first free library open to the public in the United States. The Rey Children's Room is a wonderful space that features story hours, puppet shows, sing-alongs, and other special activities throughout the year. In addition to the main library, there are twenty-seven neighborhood branches, and there is always something going on at one of them. Visit the main website for calendar listings.

Museums & Other Attractions

African Meeting House/Museum of African-American History
46 Joy Street, Boston
617-725-0022 | www.afroammuseum.org
Monday–Saturday, 10AM–4PM. Sunday, 1PM-5PM
Adults, $5; ages 13–17, $3; under 12, free.

P America's oldest standing African-American church was built in 1806.

It was an important nineteenth-century center for the black community of Boston and was sometimes called Black Faneuil Hall. The New England Anti-Slavery Society was founded here in 1832. Check their website for wonderful special programs, including meeting children's book authors, actors portraying famous abolitionists, and Kwanzaa events.

Boston Children's Museum

308 Congress Street, Boston
617-426-6500 | www.bostonkids.org
Daily, 10AM–5PM; Friday until 9PM.
Adults, $12; children 1–15, $12; under 1, free.
Friday nights are Family Dollar Night. Admission is $1 per person from 5PM to 9PM. Family memberships are available from $125; caregivers can be added for an additional $10. Membership includes admission to additional children's museums around the country.

A Numerous exhibits from the Art Studio to Arthur's Friends to the Construction Zone can keep kids entertained for hours. Head to the Playspace if you have children under age three and want to get away from the bigger kids for a while (open Saturday–Thursday, 10AM–4:30PM; Friday, 10AM–8:30PM). There's a tree house climber, a toy train landscape, and a cushioned infant area. The Family Resource Room offers parenting information and reading materials.

If you find that your family visits the museum all the time, consider a membership. This might be the best deal in town. Throughout the week, the museum offers music, art, and cooking classes specifically for the younger set. Also, make sure you check the KidStage for pint-sized productions your toddler and preschooler are sure to enjoy. See the events calendar for more information.

Boston Fire Museum

344 Congress Street, Boston
617-338-9700 | www.bostonfiremuseum.com
May–November, Saturday, 11AM–6PM.
Free.

P Since most kids adore fire engines, a Saturday visit to see the antique fire equipment and photos in this 1891 firehouse could be considered as fun as going to a candy store. The museum, which formerly housed Engine Companies 38 and 39, and later Engine 39 and Ladder 18, even allows children to play with and climb on some of the equipment. Make sure you show your little one the jewel of the collection—a hand-drawn, hand-operated pumper put into in service in 1793.

Franklin Park Zoo

1 Franklin Park Road, Boston
617-541-5466 | www.zoonewengland.com
April–September, daily, 10AM–5PM; Saturday–Sunday until 6PM; October–March, daily, 10AM–4PM.
Adults, $16; children 2–12, $10; under 2, free.
Half-price the first Saturday of the month between 10AM and noon.
Family memberships range from $70 to $100; memberships include free or discounted admission to one hundred forty zoos around the country, including the five in Massachusetts.

A Lions, tigers, and giraffes—yes, the zoo has them all! In addition, the Franklin Farm exhibit is always a big hit with kids. Children can pet cows and goats and check out baby chicks. The Butterfly Landing, open only in the summer, has more than a thousand butterflies to gaze at in wonder. The Tropical Rainforest is home to seven lowland gorillas. Special events include the Zoo Howl in October, when kids can go along a trick-or-treat trail through the zoo, and sing-alongs and other activities in the winter months.

Institute of Contemporary Art

100 Northern Avenue, Boston
617-478-3100 | www.icaboston.org
Tuesday, Wednesday, Saturday, and Sunday, 10AM–5PM; Thursday–Friday until 9PM.
Adults, $15; under 17, free.
Free on Thursdays after 5PM.
Free for families (up to two adults accompanied by children twelve and under) on the last Saturday of each month.
Family membership is $95; membership includes invitation to annual family event and discounts to family programs.

T Believe it or not, this gorgeous new museum is a wonderful spot to take the kids, especially for its Play Date program, held on the last Saturday of each month. Families get in free, and the entire day is packed with everything from films, performance, art-making activities, and gallery tours—all of which is tailored to an ongoing exhibit. Word to the wise: get there early! It can get very crowded. The setting on the waterfront is stunning. Kids will love running around outside and up and down the stairs while you watch the activity in the harbor.

Isabella Stewart Gardner Museum
280 The Fenway, Boston
617-566-1401 | www.gardnermuseum.org
Tuesday–Sunday, 11AM–5PM.
Adults, $12; under 18 or named Isabella, free.
If you visit the Gardner and the Museum of Fine Arts in a two-day period, you can get $2 off admission at either museum.

P The Gardner Museum is a time capsule, and it remains exactly as it was when Isabella Stewart Gardner died in 1924. It might not seem the best museum for kids, but pick up the family guides available at the information desk on your way in and you'll have intriguing rhymes to repeat, a treasure hunt, and culture all rolled into one. Check the website for the occasional family themed events throughout the year, such as arts and crafts, period music concerts, and dance recitals.

John F. Kennedy Library and Museum
Columbia Point, Boston
617-514-1600 | www.jfklibrary.org
Daily, 9AM–5PM.
Adults, $12; children 13–17, $9; under 12, free.

P The John F. Kennedy Presidential Library and Museum portrays the life, leadership, and legacy of President Kennedy in a breathtaking waterfront location. A replica of the Oval Office is one of the exhibits dedicated to the thirty-fifth president. Although much of the museum's content is targeted for adults and older children, preschoolers may enjoy the mock-ups. In addition, a popular program for families is the Celebrate! arts series, which is offered about once a month. The free one-hour program focuses on arts, music, and culture.

Museum of Fine Arts

465 Huntington Avenue, Boston
617-267-9300 | www.mfa.org
Daily, 10AM–4:45PM; Wednesday–Friday until 9:45PM.
Adults, $22; children 7–17, $10.50 until 3PM (after 3PM, free); under 6, free.
Your ticket allows you to visit twice in a ten-day period. After 4PM on
Wednesday, admission is by voluntary contribution.
Family memberships start at $100.

T The Museum of Fine Arts (MFA) is huge and can be intimidating to the uninitiated and the very small. Rather than aimlessly dragging your kids around in an effort to find something that interests them, go online to download self-guided activity sheets (or pick one up at the information center). Depending on your child, you might choose Mythical Creatures or Cats, among other topics. Keep an eye open for the Family Art Cart on weekends from 11AM to 4PM, when kids can learn about ancient Egyptian mysteries, read stories from Southeast Asia, or go through the museum with a set of Art Cards, looking for animals, treasures, and children in the artwork.

If you decide to head off on your own, it's a good idea to have a game plan in mind. Pick two or three exhibits that you want to visit, then call it quits. Nobody likes a cranky kid in a museum—especially mom and dad! The Egyptian Gallery is a no-brainer; kids always love the mummies. The Modern Art Gallery can make for interesting discussions with your young art critic. The Art of Africa Gallery fascinates children with beautiful masks. Keep in mind that as your young ones grow, they can really take advantage of all the MFA has to offer. After-school programs, 3:30PM–4:45PM (weekdays only), for children ages six through twelve are available on a drop-in basis during the school year. Your future artist—or art historian—will explore the MFA's different galleries and do exciting and reflective projects with museum staff. The program is free—but getting your kids hooked on art for the rest of their lives is priceless!

Museum of Science

Science Park, Boston
617-723-2500 | www.mos.org
Daily, 9AM–5PM; Friday until 9PM; July–Labor Day, 9AM–7PM.

Adults, $22; children 3–11, $19; under 3, free.
Mugar Omni Theater, Planetarium, Laser Shows, and Butterfly Garden are
extra. Family memberships start at $80.

A First stop for small kids (up to eight years): the Discovery Center. Exhibits range from dinosaur bone replicas to real, live guinea pigs. Kids are free to roam around and learn a little more about science and the natural world as they move from one station to the next. Tots can stay put at the arts activity center, splash around at the water table, climb all over the place, and play with the best building blocks parents have ever seen—they're made of foam! One section of the Discovery Center is designated as an infant-only area. Toddlers on up will enjoy the other parts of the museum as well. The Butterfly Garden is always a huge hit, and if your child needs to burn off a little extra energy, trot over to the Science in the Park exhibit. Make sure to hit the Theater of Electricity and don't forget to check out a live animal presentation as well!

New England Aquarium
Central Wharf, Boston
617-973-5200 | www.neaq.org
Monday–Friday, 9AM–5PM; Saturday–Sunday until 6PM.
Adults, $22.95; children 3–11, $15.95; under 3, free.
Family memberships start at $135.

A We always find the aquarium a soothing, mysterious place. We talk a little more softly in here, wander the darkened halls, and stare, awe-stricken at the beautiful creatures behind illuminated tanks. Our all-time favorite is the aquarium's centerpiece: the giant ocean tank. The two-hundred-thousand-gallon tank, formally named the Caribbean Coral Reef Exhibit, is a twenty-four-foot-deep reef filled with caves, reefs, sharks, turtles, and hundreds of tropical fish. A winding ramp leads up around the tank, and visitors can peek in windows as they stroll up four stories to the top. Smaller children will love the tide pool exhibit, where they can get wet and hold starfish.

Special activities such as playing with sea lions are available for an additional cost, but watching the penguins for hours is included in the price of admission. On the first and third Monday of every month, the aquarium hosts Aqua Kids Family Days. Stories, art, and live animal presentations are specifically geared toward young children in the Curious George Discovery Center. Also, the aquarium offers whale watches and harbor tours right in Boston's own backyard—the Atlantic Ocean!

Old South Meeting House

310 Washington Street, Boston
617-482-6439 | www.oldsouthmeetinghouse.org
April–October, daily, 9:30AM–5PM; November–March, daily, 10AM–4PM.
Adults, $6; children 6-18, $1, under 6, free.

P This is where it all began. At least, this is where the famous Boston Tea Party began. In 1773, five thousand colonists, angry over taxes and the Boston Massacre, raced out of the meeting hall down to the harbor and dumped three shiploads of tea into the water. Of course, it took a couple more years and a few acts of defiance before the British attempted to put those upstart colonists in their place. (*Psst ...* They didn't succeed!)

The Meeting House was built in 1729 and was the largest building in Boston at the time. A state-of-the-art audio tour will transport you and your little one back in time. You can ask for a family scavenger hunt kit that is geared toward your child's age. Or request the Anna's World Activity Kit, which is filled with hands-on objects and activities that explore the eighteenth-century meeting house through the eyes of twelve-year-old congregation member Anna Green Winslow. If that doesn't strike your fancy, come by for a re-enactment of the famous debates. Check the website for these special programs, which usually coincide with holidays and school breaks.

Deals & Free Admission Days

Boston Children's Museum
308 Congress Street, Boston
617-426-6500 | www.bostonkids.org
Friday nights are Family Dollar Night. Admission is $1 per person.
from 5PM–9PM.

Boston Fire Museum
344 Congress Street, Boston
617-482-1344 | www.bostonfiremuseum.com
May–November, Saturdays, 11AM–4PM.
Free.

Franklin Park Zoo
1 Franklin Park Road, Boston
617-541-5466 | www.zoonewengland.com
Half-price the first Saturday of the month between 10AM and noon.

Harvard Museum of Natural History
26 Oxford Street, Cambridge
617-495-3045 | www.hmnh.harvard.edu
Free to Massachusetts residents September–May,
Wednesday, 3PM–5PM; Sundays, 9AM–noon.

Institute of Contemporary Art
100 Northern Avenue, Boston
617-478-3100 | www.icaboston.org
Free for children under age seventeen.
Free for adults, Thursdays, 5PM–9PM.
Free for families (up to two adults accompanied by children twelve and under) on the last Saturday of each month.

MIT Museum
265 Massachusetts Avenue, Cambridge
617-253-5927 | www.web.mit.edu/museum
Free, Sundays, 10AM–noon.

Museum of Fine Arts
465 Huntington Avenue, Boston
617-267-9300 | www.mfa.org
Kids are always free. After 4PM on Wednesdays, admission by donation.

USS Constitution and Museum
Charlestown Navy Yard
617-426-1812 | www.ussconstitutionmuseum.org
Admission by donation.

Old State House

Corner of State and Washington streets, Boston
617-720-1713 | www.bostonhistory.org
Daily, 9AM–5PM; January, daily, 9AM–4PM; July–August, daily, 9AM–6PM.
Adults, $7.50; children 6–18, $3; under 5, free.

P The Old State House is Boston's oldest public building. The 1713 building was, at first, home to the British government; later it was the first place the Declaration of Independence was read aloud in Massachusetts. Every Fourth of July, the Declaration is read from the same balcony. At one time, there was a plan to move the Old State House to Chicago's World Fair. Of course, no self-respecting Bostonian was going to allow that to happen. In 1879, the Antiquarian Club was formed to stop it from happening. The club evolved into the Bostonian Society, which to this day maintains extensive collections documenting all periods of the city's history.

Have your kids look for the lion and the unicorn sculptures outside, which represented British royal authority. The cobblestone circle outside the building marks the Boston Massacre site. The Boston Massacre was the killing of five colonists by British soldiers on March 5, 1770. It was the culmination of civilian-military tensions that had been growing since royal troops first appeared in Massachusetts to enforce the heavy tax burden imposed by the Townshend Acts almost three years earlier.

The younger set will like the permanent exhibit *A Hands on History*, which gives kids the chance to recreate the Old State House's walls with foam bricks, peek behind the doors of the building's façade, and meet Otis, the Old State House's resident mouse.

Paul Revere House

19 North Square, Boston
617-523-2338 | www.paulreverehouse.org
Mid-April–October, daily, 9:30AM–5:15PM; November–April 14, daily, 9:30AM–4:15PM; closed Mondays, January–March.
Adults, $3.50; children 5–17, $1.

Listen, my children, and you shall hear
Of the midnight ride of Paul Revere ...

P From 1770 through 1800 Paul Revere owned this house, now the oldest remaining building in the downtown area. It was built around 1680, and much of the original building is intact. Truthfully, just walking through the house is not very interesting to small kids, but if you schedule your visit to coincide with one of the many events held throughout the year at the museum, it's a different story. Programs about life in colonial Boston, held every Saturday, May through October, can really charm the little ones. You'd be surprised how fascinated children are by these events, where everything from cutting silhouettes to music of the day is presented. Occasionally actors portray Revere, his wife, his mother-in-law, and others and will answer questions about their roles during the Revolutionary War. Check the website for various events and programs.

Sports Museum of New England
On the fifth and sixth floors of the TD Garden
Causeway Street, Boston
617-624-1234 | www.sportsmuseum.org
Schedule depends on TD Garden events. Always call before going. Generally open daily, 11AM–5PM. Admission is granted on the hour until 3PM (last entry).
Adults, $10; children 10–18, $5; under 10, free.
Buy your tickets at the TD Garden box office.

P This is an essential stop for the pint-sized sports fan in the family. Exhibits explore New England's historical highlights of everything boxing, hockey, football, basketball, soccer, and baseball. Watch old footage of the Boston Garden (true fans still lament its demise, but you can sit in old Garden seats at least!), and learn about local high school and college teams. Don't miss the Boston Bruins Hall of Fame portraits or the exhibit on the Boston Marathon.

USS *Constitution* and Museum
Charlestown Navy Yard, Boston
617-426-1812 | www.ussconstitutionmuseum.org
USS *Constitution:* April-October, 9AM-6PM;
November-March, 10AM-5PM.
Museum: Daily, April 15–November, 9AM–6PM;
November–April 14, 10AM-5PM.
Admission by donation.

P Old Ironsides, as the oldest commissioned warship afloat is affectionately called, makes its home at the Charlestown Navy Yard. If you ever get a chance to see the ship out in the harbor on the Fourth of July, it's a sight you and your kids will never forget. Crew members give daily tours of the vessel every half-hour. The ship was built in 1797 and is most famous for fighting off five British ships in the War of 1812. After the tour, visit the nearby museum for exhibits, hands-on activities, and artifacts detailing the long history of the warship.

No visit is complete without a walk around the Navy Yard. Now part of the park system, the Charlestown Navy Yard was one of the first shipyards built in the United States and remained a thriving shipyard for 174 years. Prior to that, the British landed here before the Battle of Bunker Hill. You can visit the nearby Bunker Hill Monument (Monument Square, 617-242-5641; open daily, 9AM–4:30PM) and climb up the 221-foot-high monument (294 steps) to get great views of the city, but make sure your kids can handle it, or you'll be stuck carrying them! Go to the Bunker Hill Pavilion to learn more about the battle in *Whites of Their Eyes*, a film named after the legend that the colonists weren't supposed to fire until they saw the whites of the Redcoats' eyes.

Live Theater

Boston Children's Theatre
Studios: 316 Huntington Avenue, Boston
Performances: 527 Tremont Street, Boston
617-424-6634 | www.bostonchildrenstheatre.org

P "Live Theater for Children by Children" is the motto of the Boston Children's Theatre, a seventy-five-year-old institution. Students in grades four to twelve perform productions such as *Annie*, *The Wizard of Oz*, and *The House at Pooh Corner*. The BCT also offers classes to students in kindergarten to twelfth grade. Performances are geared to ages four and up. Most children are natural performers, and getting a chance to watch their peers in action often fascinates them.

Riverside Theatre Works

45 Fairmount Avenue, Hyde Park
617-361-7024 | www.riversidetheatreworks.org

P The non-profit Riverside Theatre Works puts on several family-friendly shows a year in an intimate venue in Hyde Park and uses lots of local kids in the productions. Recent performances include *Miracle on 34th Street*, *Hansel and Gretel*, and *Willy Wonka*.

Wheelock Family Theatre

200 The Riverway, Boston (Wheelock College)
617-879-2300 | www.wheelock.edu/wft
Three mainstage productions annually.

P Wheelock Family Theatre focuses on shows that everyone can enjoy. Past productions include *Seussical* and *Charlotte's Web*. The theater works hard to attract all ages and annually offers one drama for adults, a musical, and a show for both children and adults. Classes for kindergartners on up include dance, beginning Shakespeare, puppetry and drama, and much more. Visit the website to see what is on offer during any given semester.

Music

Boston Lyric Opera

Various locations
617-542-4912 | www.blo.org

P The Boston Lyric Opera does at least one Family Day at the Opera show every season. Shows are staged in an hour and sung in English so the smallest kids will enjoy it. Performances are held at several locations around town. Afterwards the performers speak with the children about the production. Even adults wary of the opera should give this a chance! Visit the BLO website for details on venues and times, as well as interactive activities and articles to help you prepare for the performance.

Boston Symphony Orchestra/Boston Pops Orchestra
Symphony Hall
301 Massachusetts Avenue, Boston
617-266-1492 | www.bso.org

P The Boston Symphony Youth and Family Concerts are a fabulous introduction to the symphony for children. These concerts are also a bargain for music-loving parents, with much lower ticket prices than regular performances. After the show, tours of Symphony Hall are given, and pre- and post-concert activities include instrument demonstrations.

Barely Beyond Boston: Other Great Museums & Attractions

Museums

Harvard Museum of Natural History
26 Oxford Street, Cambridge
617-495-3045 | www.hmnh.harvard.edu
Daily, 9AM–5PM.
Adults, $9; children 3–18, $6; under 3, free.
Free to Massachusetts residents September–May, Wednesday, 3PM–5PM; Sunday, 9AM–noon.

P This is one of Boston's hidden treasures. The Harvard Museum of Natural History shares the building with the Botanical Museum, the Museum of Comparative Zoology, and the Mineralogical and Geological Museum (admission covers all, plus the Peabody Museum of Archaeology and Ethnology—not always a big kid hit, so it's safe to skip it).

Sheer numbers are what you get here: 3,000 glass flowers, a 1,642-pound amethyst, a 42-foot-long prehistoric marine reptile, and so on. The vast amount of taxidermic animals ("statues" for our young animal lover) is unbelievable. Nature story times are held Saturday and Sunday, usually at 11AM and 2PM.

MIT Museum

265 Massachusetts Avenue, Cambridge
617-253-4444 | www.web.mit.edu/museum
Daily, 10AM–5PM.
Adults, $7.50; children, $3; under 5, free. Sunday, free from 10AM–noon.

P The Massachusetts Institute of Technology's museum has the world's largest collection of holography. If your kids have ever found a hologram in a cereal box and thought it was cool, wait until they see these! But holograms are really the tip of the iceberg at this interactive museum, which has all sorts of cutting-edge technology displays. Hands-on is the order of the day here. Kids can check out what MIT students and professors are up to in the Innovation Gallery, with rotating installations of recent inventions. And no one can fail to be fascinated by the *Robots and Beyond* exhibit, where you can see Kismet, the world's first sociable robot. The museum offers family programs throughout the year, such as the Cambridge Science Festival in the spring, and special school vacation activities. Check their website for event details.

Museum of Transportation

Larz Anderson Park
15 Newton Street, Brookline
617-522-6547 | www.larzanderson.org
Tuesday–Sunday, 10AM–4PM.
Adults, $10; children 6–18, $5; under 6, free.
Family memberships start at $50.

P The centerpiece of Brookline's Larz Anderson Park is the Museum of Transportation, which opened in 1949. The core of the museum is the original stable of early automobiles donated to the city of Boston as part of the Larz Anderson estate and housed in the original carriage house, which was built in 1888 and is on the National Register of Historical Places. While the rotating exhibits upstairs are strictly off-limits to little fingers, the downstairs is devoted exclusively to tiny car-lovers and (other than a large collection of vintage and rare automobile toys) allows for interaction. Through spring, summer, and fall there are also weekly Sunday lawn events, free with museum admission.

Live Theater

Coolidge Corner Movie Theatre (Children's Programs)

290 Harvard Street, Brookline
617-734-2501 | www.coolidge.org
October–March, Saturday, 10:30AM.
Live shows are $8; movies, $3.

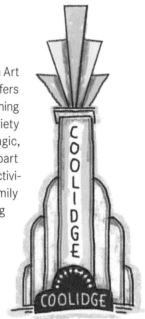

P The Coolidge, Boston's only remaining open Art Deco movie theater, which is also non-profit, offers a nice change of pace from regular Saturday morning cartoons at home. Every Saturday a family variety show is offered—and it's not just movies. Magic, dance, puppets, and classic cartoons are all part of the mix. Another one of my family's favorite activities is to go to the occasional interactive family movies at the Coolidge. Similar in feel to going to the *Rocky Horror Picture Show*, movies such as *The Princess Bride* are awesome when everyone in the packed audience is quoting the movie, brandishing blow-up swords, and ringing bells (all provided by the theater).

Magic Ark Children's Series

Leventhal-Sidman Jewish Community Center
333 Nahanton Street, Newton
617-558-6522 | www.lsjcc.org
Admission is $9.

T The Magic Ark Children's Series, usually offered on Sundays, showcases family entertainers, touring acts, and local performers. Catch a popular singer, such as Steve Roslonek of *StevesSongs*; a book brought to life, such as *Nate the Great*; or jugglers and circus acts, among others. All shows are open to the community at large; you don't need to be a JCC member.

Puppet Showplace Theatre

32 Station Street, Brookline
617-731-6400 | www.puppetshowplace.org
Performances during the school year: Saturday and Sunday, 1PM and 3PM; preschool show, Thursday, 10:30AM.
Summer performances: Wednesday and Thursday, 10:30AM and 1PM.
Daily performances during school breaks.
Admission is $10 per person for Family Shows.

P The Puppet Showplace Theatre is a magical experience, but make sure your kids are up for it. Some smaller children are afraid of puppets. Weekend shows are for kids five years of age and older. Special Tot shows on Thursdays are targeted for ages three to five years, where the puppeteers introduce themselves and the stories are more familiar. The theater is small, with less than one hundred seats. No seat is bad, but make sure you get one by reserving well in advance. A recent lineup of shows included *Cinderella*, *Peter Rabbit*, and *Puss in Boots*. After the show, the puppeteers will often allow children a closer look at the puppets, and sometimes (for a fee) you can make your own.

Note: *Tickets sell out regularly, be sure to book in advance.*

Regent Theatre

7 Medford Street, Arlington
781-646-4849 | www.regenttheatre.com
Adults, $10; children, $8.

T This former vaudeville house has just five hundred seats, making it a perfect venue for its Family Fun Saturday Shows at 10:30AM. These popular one-hour shows have featured everyone from singer Ben Rudnick to Jenny the Juggler and many other kid-pleasing performers. The shows are not weekly, so check the website for current listings.

Note: *Tickets sell out quickly, be sure to book immediately after a show is announced.*

Top 10 Family Adventures in Boston

Deirdre Wilson, senior editor of the *Boston Parents' Paper*, a monthly magazine serving Eastern Massachusetts, and author of *The Lobster Kids' Guide to Exploring Boston* (Lobster Press, 2001), shares these Beantown family adventures:

1. **Make Way for Ducklings** sculptures at Boston's Public Garden, where author Robert McCloskey's book of the same name comes to life. Kids love to sit on the backs of the Mallard family depicted in the book.

2. **A Boston Duck Tour** on a World War II amphibious landing vehicle is good for sightseeing, Boston trivia, and plenty of laughs. Eventually, these vehicles splash into the Charles River for waterside views of Boston—and sometimes child passengers are chosen to man the steering wheel for a while.

3. In early June, we head to City Hall Plaza off Congress Street for the annual **Scooper Bowl** where you can sample ice cream from top manufacturers—all for one small fee that benefits the Jimmy Fund.

4. **Faneuil Hall** is my children's hands-down favorite place to visit in Boston. We love to watch street performers, grab a slice of pizza, and sit outside for some fantastic people watching.

5. The **Museum of Science** is probably the number one choice for area families. My kids' favorite exhibits include the star shows at the Planetarium and the lightning demonstrations in the Theater of Electricity.

6. The **Boston Children's Museum** offers hours of fun for the young (and young at heart). Try the netted, tubular climbing structure, the *Construction Zone*, and the amazing *Kid Power* exhibits.

7. Gaze into seals' and sea lions' deep brown eyes from the decks of the open-air exhibit space at the **New England Aquarium**.

8. At the **Franklin Park Zoo**, my girls adore the gorilla exhibit because its huge floor-to-ceiling display windows allow you to get up close and personal with the hairy beasts.

9. The **Skywalk Observatory** on the fiftieth floor of the Prudential Center offers 360-degree views of the city and beyond. Take the audio tour to see and learn about key historic and cultural sites in the city.

10. Tour the **USS *Constitution*** with U.S. Navy sailors, where you can stand at the huge steering wheel, run your hands over the cannons, and explore the officers' quarters below deck. Across the street at the museum, kids love operating the steering wheel, hoisting sails, and firing cannons.

◈9◈ Get Outta Town!

Fun day trips for a family on the go

READY FOR A little adventure? Starting from the North Shore, you can access amazing New England destinations for a day trip or a longer getaway. Think: Maine, New Hampshire, Vermont, Martha's Vineyard, Nantucket, Newport, Mystic Seaport, and even the Big Apple!

Here are some tried and true favorite family-friendly destinations, with suggestions for when to pack the kids into the car and hit the open road!

Fall

Ben & Jerry's Factory Tours

1281 Waterbury-Stowe Road, Waterbury, Vermont
802-882-1240 | www.benjerry.com
Seven days a week, year-round, except certain holidays. See the website for details.
Adults, $3; 12 and under, free.

A Take a drive to Vermont for a little leaf peeping, and stop in at the Ben & Jerry's factory for a thirty-minute guided tour, where you'll learn how the ice cream is produced, and how the company's philosophy is incorporated into day-to-day business. And, of course, you'll get to indulge in samples! Tours are room-temperature and stroller-friendly.

ECHO Lake Aquarium and Science Center

1 College Street, Burlington, Vermont
802-864-1848 | www.echovermont.org
Year-round, 10AM–5PM, except Thanksgiving and Christmas Eve and Day.
Adults, $12.50; children from 3-17, $9.50; kids 2 and under, free. (Note: full-day parking in the ECHO lot is $8.)

A The ECHO Lake Aquarium and Science Center has a seven-thousand-gallon aquarium featuring some of the biggest fish of Lake Champlain. Permanent exhibits include a water playspace for kids to build dams and float boats, and an Atlantic tide pool touch tank with snails, crabs, sea stars, anemones, and sea urchins. There's a working miniature lighthouse for small kids, an exhibit on frogs, and much more.

Winter

The Children's Museum of New Hampshire

6 Washington Street, Dover, New Hampshire
603-742-2002 | www.childrens-museum.org
Monday–Saturday, 10AM–5PM; Sundays, noon–5PM;
closed Mondays during the school year except for
school vacation weeks and selected holidays.
Adults and children over 1, $9.

A At this museum, kids can engineer their own flying machines, step into a story, become paleontologists, play post office, board a submarine, and so much more. The museum does not serve food but offers a 1950s-style snack area where families can take a quick break. You can bring your own snacks or purchase some healthy options from the vending machines. Note that the use of strollers is not recommended inside the museum; strollers can be parked in the coat room off the entryway. Two backpacks and an infant front carrier are available at the front desk for parents to use on a complimentary first-come, first-served basis.

Discovery Museum

177 Main Street, Acton, Massachusetts
978-264-4200 | www.discoverymuseums.org
See website for hours and school-year schedules for both museums.
Adults and children, $10.50.

A Discovery Museum has two small museums on the same campus. At the Children's Discovery Center, geared toward toddlers through children in early grade school, kids can surround themselves with a bubble wall, be a train conductor, and choose from many hands-on exhibits. The Science Discovery Museum, for older kids, features hands-on science exhibits where kids can learn about concepts like sound waves and vortexes. There are picnic tables on the grounds for nice weather, and plenty of nearby restaurants.

The Hobo Railroad

Lincoln, New Hampshire
603-745-2135 | www.hoborr.com
Adults, $14; children from 3-11, $10; children two and under ride free.

A The Hobo Railroad features an eighty-minute train ride along the Pemigewasset River in vintage cars. As you travel, you can enjoy treats like a hobo picnic lunch or ice cream. Trains run rain or shine. See the website for train schedules. In the winter, there's also a Santa Express ride that includes free hot chocolate and cookies, plus a visit from Mr. Claus, who has a gift for everyone. (Special event tickets are $15 for coach; $18, first class.)

The Polar Express Journey to the North Pole Event

Believe in Books Literacy Foundation, PO Box 1800
Lincoln and North Conway, New Hampshire
603-356-9980 | www.polarexpress.org
Coach, $45; first class, $55; dome and premier, $65.

A Travel to the North Pole just like the children from *The Polar Express* on this beautiful two-hour train ride through the White Mountains. The trip includes hot chocolate and a visit from Santa and his elves, and a walk to the North Pole Theater, where the little boy from the book (who has miraculously stayed the same age) will read *The Polar Express*. Because of extreme popularity, tickets are available through a mail-in lottery system and must include a non-refundable $10 donation, which is tax deductible. (The organization is a 501(c)(3) non-profit corporation.) Limited ticket packages are also available through lodging sponsors. See the website for details.

Santa's Village

Route 2, Jefferson, New Hampshire
603-586-4445 | www.santasvillage.com
See website calendar for days and hours of operation.
Ages 4 and up, $26; children 3 and under, free.

A It's Christmas all year at this "village of family fun!" Let the kids enjoy the rides, games, live shows, and activities such as petting Santa's reindeer, visiting with the big guy himself, and decorating gingerbread cookies. Mary and Joseph's Nursery has changing spots available, plus a separate room for nursing moms who want more privacy. Food is available.

Spring

Dinosaur State Park

400 West Street, Rocky Hill, Connecticut
860-529-8423 | www.dinosaurstatepark.org
Year-round, Tuesday–Sunday, 9AM–4:30PM; closed Mondays and holidays.
Ages 13 and over, $6; 6-12, $2; 5 and under, free.

A Dinosaur State Park officially opened in 1968, two years after two thousand dinosaur tracks were accidentally uncovered during excavation for a new state building. Five hundred of the tracks are now enclosed within the Exhibit Center's geodesic dome. The park also features interactive displays, life-size dioramas, nature trails, and more.

Mystic Seaport

75 Greenmanville Avenue, Mystic, Connecticut
860-572-5339 | www.mysticseaport.org

See the website for calendar of events and hours of operation.
Adults, $24; children 6-17, $15; kids 5 and under, free.

A Mystic Seaport promises to tucker out your kids ages seven and under! At their Children's Museum, young sailors can swab the deck, move cargo, cook in the galley, dress in sailors' garb, and even catch some shuteye in the ships' bunks. On Saturdays and Sundays during the winter months (December–March), there's a free one-hour story time geared toward kids ages four to seven. There are restaurants on the premises, plus an area for picnics, including a Wooden Boats Playground for kids.

Old Sturbridge Village

1 Old Sturbridge Village Road, Sturbridge, Massachusetts
800-733-1830 | www.osv.org
See website for hours of operation.
Adults, $20; children 3-17, $7; under 3, free.

A At this early nineteenth-century New England village, kids can learn all about New England life from 1790–1840. Take the family for a ride in a stagecoach (or for a horse-drawn sleigh ride on winter weekends), meet the farm animals, and take part in hands-on crafts. There are several dining options to feed your little historians, including a café, a cafeteria, and a tavern. Picnic tables are also available, and you're welcome to bring your own lunch. Strollers are available for rent.

Roger Williams Zoo

1000 Elmwood Avenue, Providence, Rhode Island
401-785-3510 | www.rogerwilliamsparkzoo.org
Year-round, daily, 9AM–4PM (last admission at 3:30PM); closed for some holidays and special events.
Adults, $12; children ages 3- 12, $8; under three, free.

A Take your family on safari, visit a rainforest, and discover the land down under. The Roger Williams Zoo features over 160 different species of animals, all roaming in natural settings. For a separate fee, classes and programs are available for toddlers and preschoolers to learn about wildlife. The classes are generally an hour long and include snacks, music, arts, crafts, and stories. (Registration is required.) Strollers and double strollers are available for rent. Restrooms and baby changing and nursing facilities are available throughout the zoo. There are two restaurants at the zoo, plus mobile food carts located throughout. One tip: storage lockers are not available, so be prepared to play Sherpa if you bring too much.

Summer

Canobie Lake Park
Route 93, Exit 2 or 3, Salem, New Hampshire
603-893-3506 | www.canobie.com
April–September. See website for hours, which are subject to change.
General admission, $30; under 48 inches (or over 60 years), $21; after 5PM, $20 for everyone; ages 3 and under, free.

T **P** **E** Canobie Lake Park is totally doable for families with a variety of ages in their pack. There's a great selection of rides for the wee ones and plenty to keep parents and older kids happy too. Not to mention all the food options—*yum*! Additionally, strollers and lockers are available for rent, and there are some beautiful green spaces along the water. There's a nursing room for breastfeeding moms, and bathrooms are equipped with changing tables. The parking is free, and this is one day trip that all but guarantees sleeping kids on the ride home.

Davis Farmland
145 Redstone Hill Road, Sterling, Massachusetts
978-422-6666 | www.davisfarmland.com
See the website for hours of operation and admission prices, which change with the weather and seasons.

A The Davis Farmland Children's Discovery Museum promises hands-on family fun, featuring endangered farm animals and learning. In the spring, kids can become a junior farmer for the day by helping out with milking, egg collecting, and bottle feeding animals. There's also a kiddie maze, a bouncy house, swings, and pony and hayrides. In the summer months, there's a fantastic spray park, with geysers and misters and even a kiddie car wash. Families can pick their own pumpkins and apples in autumn. If you have some older kids, check out the Davis Mega Maze, a giant 3-D adventure cornfield maze. After you visit the farm, head over to Texas Roadhouse for dinner, where families coming from Davis Farmland get 10 percent off their dinner bill. *Whoopee!*

EcoTarium

222 Harrington Way, Worcester, Massachusetts
508-929-2700 | www.ecotarium.org
Year-round (excluding holidays), Tuesday–Saturday, 10AM–5PM; Sundays, noon–5PM; closed Mondays.
Adults, $12; children ages 2-18, $8; under 2, free.

A The EcoTarium is an indoor-outdoor museum focused on science and nature. Inside, three floors of exhibits teach children about natural history, wildlife, and our planet's history. Outside, there's a variety of animal exhibits—from frogs to polar bears, chinchillas to turtles. (Check the website for animal encounters program schedules, where kids can get up close and personal with these creatures.) Kids over seven can try the Tree Canopy Walkway, a series of platforms and rope bridges suspended forty feet above ground in a grove of oak and hickory trees. (Little daredevils will zip down on a harness after their treetop exploration.) If you have a little guy who loves trains, you won't want to miss the Explorer Express Train, which is an additional $3. There's also an extra fee for the planetarium ($5) and the Tree Canopy Walkway ($10), which is seasonal. If you have a good time in the summer, consider heading back to the EcoTarium when the holidays come for their Polar Bear's Journey holiday program for young kids.

Mount Washington Cog Railway

Base Road, six miles off Route 302, Bretton Woods, New Hampshire
800-922-8825 | www.thecog.com
Weekends only in May; daily, June–October. See website for train schedules.
Adults, $62; children 4-12, $39; 3 and under, free on adult's lap; seniors, $57.

A This is an old-fashioned scenic train ride to the top of Mount Washington, the highest peak in the Northeast. The round trip to the summit takes three hours, with a one-hour stop at the top, where you can visit the state park and the Mount Washington Observatory Center and Museum. There are no restroom facilities on the train, so be sure to use the restrooms at the base station before boarding (there's a restaurant at the base station). Strollers, car seats, and coolers are not allowed on the train—carry-on items must be small enough to fit on your lap. Some trains are fired by coal, and temperatures are cooler at the summit, so be sure to dress accordingly.

Hampton Inn Water Park
1788 White Mountain Highway, North Conway, New Hampshire
603-356-7736 | www.hamptoninn.hilton.com
See website for rates.

A North Conway has always been a favorite for North Shore families because of the great tax-free shopping at Settler's Green Outlet Village, nearby Story Land, and the White Mountains Polar Express Train Ride during the holidays. Add the Hampton Inn in North Conway to the list. This hotel has an indoor water park that's perfect for smaller kids, plus free breakfast in the morning. It is a great place to stay when exploring all the area has to offer.

One Stop Fun, Inc.
49 Power Road, Westford, Massachusetts
978-692-9907 | www.onestopfun.com
Pool open weekdays 11AM–7PM; weekends, 10AM–7PM.
Adults, free; children, $15 for the pool only; after 7PM, children, $7. Daily passes available for non-members.

A One Stop Fun is great for gymnastics or free play on the indoor play structure, which has a separate toddler area. In the summer, there's a great outdoor pool that has a large toddler-friendly shallow area that's just one and a half feet deep. There are also lemon drop squirts, five water slides, a spray station playground, and water tables that kids of all ages love. Certified lifeguards are on duty at all times. There are chairs, tables with umbrellas, restrooms and outdoor showers, plus a snack shack with table service and access to an air conditioned indoor snack bar.

Southwick's Wild Animal Zoo

2 Southwick Street, Mendon, Massachusetts
800-258-9182 | www.southwickszoo.com
Mid-April–mid-October, daily, 10AM–5PM,
including holidays. Petting zoo open year-round.
Adults, $19.50; children 3-12, $13.50; kids under 2, free.

A The Southwick's Wild Animal Zoo is a family-owned zoo where you can visit animals in a naturalistic setting. There are over one hundred species of animals from all over the world. If that's not enough for your own pack of wild animals, try out the train ride, Skyfari Sky Rides, or the kiddie rides. Strollers are available for rent ($5). There are a variety of concession options available. The zoo suggests wearing comfortable shoes as it's on natural terrain.

Stone Zoo

149 Pond Street, Stoneham, Massachusetts
781-438-5100 | www.zoonewengland.org
Year-round, daily, 10AM–5PM, and weekends until 6PM.
Adults, $13; children ages 2-12, $9; under 2, free.

A The Stone Zoo is a great zoo for small children. You can bring your own picnic or purchase food at the zoo. And there are some great promotions and events: On the first Saturday of the month from 10AM to noon, everyone pays the kids' admission price ($7). Free story times are held Saturday and Sunday at 12:30PM, and animal encounters are held at 11:30AM and 1:30PM during the week.

Story Land

850 New Hampshire 16, Glen, New Hampshire
603-383-4186 | www.storylandnh.com
May–October.
Adults and children 3 and up, $27.99; active military, $24.99; under 3, free.

T **P** **E** This sweet little amusement park is a must-visit for the preschool set. Think: Disneyland on a much smaller, more manageable scale. There are plenty of toddler-sized rides and attractions, and even some rides that parents and big kids will love. If you purchase the full-price admission during the last three hours of any day (after 3PM in July and August or after 2PM in other months), you'll receive a free pass to come back the next day.

Tanglewood

297 West Street, Lenox, Massachusetts
888-266-1200 | www.bso.org
See concert season schedule online for hours and ticket pricing.
Free for kids ages 17 and under; up to 4 free children's tickets are available per parent or legal guardian per concert at the Tanglewood box office on the day of the concert.

A Drink up the culture with your family at Tanglewood. On Sundays at noon, kids can take part in music and arts and crafts supervised by BSO staff. There's also a Watch and Play program on Sunday afternoons for kids to learn about an instrument, a concert theme, or a musical concept; tickets to the Sunday performance are required, and kids must be accompanied by an adult. Tanglewood is a great place to introduce your children to the magic of music, but there are a few rules for potentially unruly audience members: children and young people admitted without charge must sit with their parent or legal guardian on the lawn, and those under age five must sit on the rear half of the lawn. (Children under five are not permitted in the Koussevitzky Music Shed or Seiji Ozawa Hall during concerts.) No matter what, this is a road trip that will give your family something to sing about!

Water Country

2300 Lafayette Road, Portsmouth, New Hampshire
603-427-1111 | www.watercountry.com
See website for operating days and hours, which are subject to change.
Under 48 inches tall, $24.99; over 48 inches tall, $37.99; children 2 and under, free. Rates are reduced after 3PM: $19.99 and $24.99, respectively.

A Take a day trip to Portsmouth during the summer to cool off at Water Country. Children under forty-eight inches who are accompanied by an adult can enjoy climbing up and sliding down the arms of Ollie Octopus, play in a pirate ship, and splash around in the Tahiti Treehouse, which has a giant tipping bucket of water. Life jackets are available free of charge at guest information located inside the park. Swim diapers for children who need them are required and available in the gift shop. You may bring food into the park, and food is available for purchase throughout the park. Changing tables are located in every bathroom.

York's Wild Kingdom Zoo and Amusement Park
Route 1, York Beach, Maine
207-363-4911 | www.yorkzoo.com
May–September. See website for hours of operation.
Zoo and ride package for adults, $21.25; kids ages 4-12, $16.25; kids 3 and under, $4.75. Zoo only for adults, $14.75; kids, $9; kids 3 and under, $1. Rides only unlimited all-day passes are $11 for all ages. Go-karts, elephant rides, and pony rides sold separately.

A Attractions include exotic animal exhibits, a butterfly kingdom, a petting zoo, rides, paddle boats, a miniature golf course, a haunted house, and more. There's a picnic area on the grounds and food available for purchase. Bring some hand sanitizer and plenty of quarters (or dollar bills for the change machines) for the petting zoo food dispensers if your children want to feed the animals. Be aware that all the rides have varying height restrictions, so if you're visiting with children in a range of heights, they may not all be able to go on the same rides. See the website for discount coupons. And don't miss the nearby Kittery outlets on your way home!

More fun ideas:

- Beech Hill Farm and Ice Cream Barn, New Hampshire

- Cape Cod Scenic Railroad, Massachusetts

- Children's Museum and Theatre of Maine

- Dr. Seuss National Memorial Sculpture Garden, Western Massachusetts

- Eric Carle Museum of Picture Book Art, Amherst, Massachusetts

- Magic Wings Butterfly Conservatory, Western Massachusetts

- The Vermont Teddy Bear Factory, Vermont

- ZooQuarium, Yarmouth, Massachusetts

Calendar of Annual Events

January

New Year's Rockport Eve
Downtown Rockport
www.newyearsrockporteve.com

New Year's Rockport Eve is a very family-friendly way to ring in the New Year. In the past, this annual event has featured live musical performances, puppet shows, clowns, raffles, contests, dancing, psychic readings, magicians, storytelling, a free train ride through the streets of Rockport, and plenty of food and hot chocolate for sale. The crowd gathers in Dock Square at midnight to sing Auld Lang Syne.

February

Salem's So Sweet
Downtown Salem
978-744-0004 | www.salem-chamber.org

The Salem Chamber of Commerce hosts an annual ice sculpture and chocolate festival, all in honor of romance. The festival is free and open to the public. Many of the downtown businesses and restaurants will be offering specials, discounts, and promotions for people coming to view the ice sculptures.

Winter Carnival
Downtown Newburyport
www.bartletmall.org

Winter Carnival is a free, fun event, held at Bartlet Mall downtown. Activities include snow volleyball, sledding, skating on the pond, snowboarding, a kids' parade, contests, hayrides, live music, and plenty of food.

June

Kite Festival

Family Service Inc. and Pemberton Park on the Merrimack River, Lawrence
978-283-1601 | www.groundworklawrence.org

Take the family for this annual festival featuring kite making (and flying!), food, music, games, face painting, trolley rides, and more.

Sand & Sea Festival

Salisbury Beach
www.beachfests.org

The annual Sand & Sea Festival at Salisbury Beach features carnival games, inflatables, face painting, sand art, youth beach soccer games, sand sculptures, dancing, live performances, contests, fireworks, and more. Many activities are free, with a small fee for some activities.

St. Peter's Fiesta

Downtown Gloucester
978-283-1601 | www.stpetersfiesta.org

This fun and often rowdy festival honors St. Peter, patron saint of fishermen. Events include the blessing of the fleet, a parade, carnival rides and games, and the notorious greasy pole competition.

Strawberry Festival

Topsfield Common
www.topsfieldhistory.org

Don't miss the Strawberry Festival in downtown Topsfield, where you'll find local farmers selling their strawberries, games for kids, arts and crafts, live music, and more.

July

Celebrate the Fourth!

You don't have to look far to find parades and fireworks scheduled to celebrate the Fourth of July all around the North Shore. Wilmington has an elaborate week-long Fourth of July celebration. Rockport has a giant thirty- to forty-foot bonfire on Back Beach. Gloucester has their annual Horribles parade and fireworks over the harbor. Don't miss Manchester's nostalgic Fourth of July parade through town and fireworks over Singing Beach.

Yankee Homecoming

Downtown Newburyport
www.yankeehomecoming.com

This week-long event features a parade, concerts, fireworks, sidewalk sales, music, food, road races, and more.

Riverfront Music Festival

Waterfront Park, behind the Firehouse Center for the Arts in Market Square, downtown Newburyport
978-462-6680 | www.newburyportchamber.org

Newburyport's acclaimed music festival features live performances from world-renowned musicians, plus free events like laser sailboat races and plenty of shopping, food, and drinks.

Marblehead Festival of Arts

www.marbleheadfestival.org

The Marblehead Festival of Arts features outdoor concerts, face painting, art exhibits, contests, games, fireworks, and more.

August

Essex Music Festival
Centennial Grove off of Centennial Grove Road, Essex
www.essexmusicfestival.com
$10 donation; kids 15 and under are free.

The Essex Music Festival features acoustic bands from bluegrass to folk and Cajun to blues. Past festivals have also included swimming, Cajun dancing, raffles, and food choices such as pulled pork sandwiches and Woodman's famous clam chowder.

Crane Beach Sandblast!
Crane Beach, 290 Argilla Road, Ipswich
978-356-4354
Spectators are welcome with regular beach admission; team fees are $7 per team plus regular beach admission.

Come to build a sand castle or just to watch the other sculptors at work. Each year, there's a different theme for the sand castles, with prizes awarded for the best sandcastles, plus family activities happening on the beach. Vote for your favorite sand castle in the People's Choice competition.

Gloucester Waterfront Festival
Stage Fort Park, Gloucester

The Gloucester Waterfront Festival features products from local artisans, live music, food, games, children's entertainment (puppets and magic shows), antique autos, and more. The event is free and is held rain or shine.

The Hamilton-Wenham Teddy Bear Picnic
Patton Park

The Hamilton-Wenham Mothers' Club hosts an annual Teddy Bear Picnic each summer at Patton Park. Children bring their favorite teddy bears to the picnic, march in a parade, and dance together to live children's music.

Salem Annual Heritage Days
Downtown Salem
www.salem-chamber.org

The Salem Annual Heritage Days is a ten-day event featuring live music, an ice cream bowl, a pizza contest, kids' day on the common, road races, bicycle races, an antique boat show, swimming events, a street fair, and more.

September

Appleton Farms Family Farm Day
219 County Road, Route 1A, Ipswich
978-356-5728 | www.thetrustees.org
10AM–3PM.

Celebrate fall with educational farm activities, music, food, pony rides, pumpkin picking, and more. Kids can see barnyard animals and can try making butter or spinning wool.

Gloucester Schooner Festival
Gloucester Harbor
www.capeannvacations.com/schooner

The Gloucester Schooner Festival is held annually during Labor Day weekend, featuring many of the last remaining schooners along the eastern seaboard, plus small craft races, a parade of boats, toy boat building for kids, food, music, and fireworks over Gloucester Harbor.

Fish Box Derby Race
Rogers Street, downtown Gloucester
www.fishboxderby.org

Every year for the past sixteen years, the Fish Box Derby has offered the kids of Cape Ann the opportunity to test their design, building, and driving skills in a safe and exciting race down Rogers Street. Kids work side by side with their parents, grandparents, guardians, or neighbors to build their own car and participate in the race. Children ages eight to fourteen are eligible to enter (there are no fees to enter), and the race is free and open to the public. The event is fun for the entire family to watch.

October

Essex ClamFest

Memorial Park on Martin Street, Essex

The Essex ClamFest, held in Memorial Park in Essex every fall, is a fun outing for the whole family. Local restaurants compete for the coveted People's Choice Award for best chowder. A $5 entry fee buys you a plastic spoon, all the chowder you can taste, and a ballot to place your vote. Non-chowder eaters will also find plenty of hot dogs, hamburgers, and lemonade stands, plus live music, goods from local artisans, and children's games (often even a pony ride).

Topsfield Fair

Route 1, Topsfield
978-887-5000 | www.topsfieldfair.org
Children under 8 are free with an adult; adults are $10 on weekdays, $12 on weekends and Columbus Day.

The oldest county fair in the nation, complete with baby pig races, horse and oxen pulling, beekeeping, farming demonstrations, the largest pumpkin contest, carnival rides, games, food, and more.

Salem's Haunted Happenings

Salem
www.hauntedhappenings.org

Salem's citywide celebration throughout the month of October features a kids' parade, haunted houses, trolley tours, a walking tour for children, and an annual Children's Day that features a costume parade, music and spooky storytelling, and more.

Pumpkin Fest

Patton Park, Hamilton
www.hwmothersclub.com

The Hamilton-Wenham Pumpkin Fest features pumpkin carving, a craft fair, a chili cook-off, games, face painting, hayrides, a costume parade, a spaghetti dinner, a bonfire, an outdoor movie, and ends with a special a pumpkin lighting event.

Rockport Harvest Festival
Downtown Rockport
978-283-1601 | www.rockportusa.com

This family-friendly event is usually held in mid-October in downtown Rockport, featuring live music, face painting, pumpkins, scarecrows, and hayrides—including all the delicious foods of autumn you can think of!

Newburyport Fall Harvest Festival
Downtown Newburyport
www.newburyportchamber.org

The Newburyport Fall Harvest Festival, typically held over Columbus Day weekend, features handmade crafts and artwork, local food vendors, live music in Market Square, an annual scarecrow contest, a teddy bear parade, and a Kid's Korner with crafts and entertainment. The event is free and open to the public.

November

Feaster Five Road Race
Brickstone Square on York Street, Andover
www.feasterfive.com

The Feaster Five is a Thanksgiving Day road race featuring a five mile course and a 5K course. Andover families love to run the Feaster Five on Thanksgiving morning so they don't have to feel quite so guilty about stuffing themselves at Thanksgiving dinner! The race is a family tradition for people of all physical levels, attracting more than seven thousand runners and walkers each year, including children, parents, and grandparents.

December

Castle Hill's Holiday Choral Concert

The Crane Estate, 290 Argilla Road, Ipswich
978-356-4351 | www.craneestate.org
$20 for members; $25 for non-members.

Take a break from the hustle and bustle of the holidays and visit Castle Hill for the annual Holiday Choral Concert. Holiday refreshments are served. Pre-registration is recommended.

Tree Lightings and Santa Visits

There are a plethora of holiday events around the North Shore where families can gather to watch tree lightings and kids can catch a glimpse of Santa Claus. Check out the Jingle Bell Walk in Manchester, Marblehead's Christmas Walk, Gloucester's Lobster Trap Tree, Rockport's Tree Lighting, and Methuen's Festival of Trees, just to name a few. Where else but on the North Shore of Boston can you see Santa travel by lobster boat to visit all the good girls and boys?

Appendix: How the Towns Stack Up

Stats on North Shore School Districts: Compiled by the Massachusetts Department of Education.

Graduation Rates for 4-Year High Schools:
[Source: The Massachusetts Department of Education
2009 Graduation Rate Report by district for 4-year schools:
http://profiles.doe.mass.edu/state_report/gradrates.aspx]

District	% Graduated
Salem Academy Charter (District)	100
Georgetown	97
North Andover	96.9
Hamilton-Wenham	96.8
Lynnfield	95.5
Andover	95
Manchester Essex Regional	94.2
Newburyport	93.4
Ipswich	89.9
Marblehead	87.7
Rockport	87.4
Danvers	85.9
Amesbury	85
Gloucester	81.7
Beverly	80.5
Peabody	78.7
Methuen	77
Salem	74.8
Lynn	70.7
Haverhill	64
Lawrence	48.1

2007-08 Per Pupil Expenditures Report
[Source: The Massachusetts Department of Education:
http://profiles.doe.mass.edu/state_report/ppx.aspx]

District	Expenditure Per Pupil
Greater Lawrence	$20,290
Salem	$13,774
Manchester Essex	$12,998
Lynn	$12,996
Lawrence	$12,643

Hamilton-Wenham	$12,616
Andover	$12,536
Newburyport	$12,199
Danvers	$12,061
Gloucester	$12,044
Peabody	$11,947
Amesbury	$11,568
Beverly	$11,488
Rockport	$11,436
Haverhill	$11,203
Marblehead	$11,133
Topsfield	$10,852
Boxford	$10,746
North Andover	$10,479
Lynnfield	$10,276
Methuen	$10,267
Ipswich	$10,186
Nahant	$9,783
Georgetown	$8,243

2006-07 SAT Report

[Source: The Massachusetts Department of Education:
http://profiles.doe.mass.edu/state_report/sat.aspx]

School	Reading	Writing	Math
Amesbury High	491	488	499
Andover High	557	551	574
Beverly High	511	500	521
Danvers High	495	493	502
Georgetown Middle/High	533	533	558
Gloucester High	500	491	496
Hamilton-Wenham Reg High	565	565	561
Haverhill High	491	476	476
Ipswich High	526	528	536
Lawrence High	395	390	406
Lynn Classical High	453	435	457
Lynn English High	446	428	444
Lynn Voc Tech Institute	376	353	382
Lynnfield High	537	550	554
Manchester Essex Reg Middle High School	540	534	550
Marblehead High	554	548	554
Methuen High	473	476	490
Newburyport High	538	539	547
North Andover High	530	524	549

Peabody Veterans Memorial High	478	479	492
Rockport High	508	506	501
Salem High	460	459	474
Saugus High	482	495	501

Average Taxes and Income by Town

Average 2009 Property Taxes of Single-Family Homes (Owner-occupied): State median: $3,573 [Source: Boston.com and the Department of Revenue: http://www.boston.com/realestate/specials/fallhousehunt/2009/property_tax_2009/]

Municipality	Amount
Manchester	$8,754
Hamilton	$7,856
Boxford	$7,612
Swampscott	$7,534
Topsfield	$7,206
Andover	$7,054
Lynnfield	$6,411
Marblehead	$6,272
Essex	$6,221
West Newbury	$6,213
North Andover	$5,896
Middleton	$5,633
Amesbury	$5,490
Nahant	$5,215
Newburyport	$5,122
Ipswich	$5,071
Beverly	$4,852
Gloucester	$4,817
Rowley	$4,633
Rockport	$4,516
Danvers	$4,391
Merrimac	$4,310
Georgetown	$4,213
Newbury	$4,203
Salem	$4,194
Groveland	$4,029
Haverhill	$3,365
Saugus	$3,332
Lynn	$3,318
Methuen	$3,248
Peabody	$3,124
Salisbury	$3,113
Lawrence	$2,269

Average 2009 Assessed Value of Single-Family Homes

Average 2009 Assessed Value of Single-Family Homes (Owner-Occupied)

[Source: Boston.com and The Department Of Revenue; Individual Communities http://www.boston.com/realestate/specials/fallhousehunt/2009/assessed_values/]

Municipality	Average Value
Manchester	$1,061,093
Marblehead	$697,696
Boxford	$647,245
Nahant	$611,363
Andover	$580,087
Lynnfield	$571,401
Topsfield	$559,503
Rockport	$536,393
Swampscott	$525,418
Essex	$522,803
Hamilton	$515,841
West Newbury	$514,340
Middleton	$512,573
Gloucester	$501,745
North Andover	$501,396
Ipswich	$490,464
Newburyport	$468,605
Newbury	$458,826
Beverly	$446,817
Georgetown	$422,140
Rowley	$408,572
Danvers	$391,693
Groveland	$367,264
Merrimac	$363,432
Saugus	$363,391
Salisbury	$339,888
Peabody	$335,932
Amesbury	$332,153
Salem	$324,588
Methuen	$300,473
Haverhill	$293,847
Lynn	$260,462
Lawrence	$212,015

About the Author

DANA ROUSMANIERE is a writer, editor, producer, and content manager for online and print publications. Dana has held positions as managing editor of FitPregnancy.com, group product manager at Lycos.com, senior producer at Lifetime Television Online, instructor for mediabistro.com, and new media editor for Hearst Publishing. She has written for *Fit Pregnancy, Good Housekeeping, The Atlantic Monthly Online, Women's Health, TripAdvisor, AOL's City's Best, Babble, Northshore*, and others. Dana lives on Boston's beautiful North Shore with her husband and three children.

About the Designer/Illustrator

HOLLY GORDON is a freelance graphic designer and digital illustrator who grew up on the North Shore. After graduating from The New England Institute of Art in Brookline in 2009, she dove into an independent career and has worked on a wide range of projects from wine events, author websites and restaurant logos to e-books and iPhone apps. Her work has recently been published by Simon & Schuster, and her food truck is a contendor on *The Food Network's* The Great Food Truck Race. Currently living in sunny Los Angeles, Holly has clients from the East Coast to the West and plans to venture into the art of letterpress. **www.missgordon.com**

About the Illustrator

RACHEL HIRSH has studied art all her life, with a strong interest in children's books. She received a BFA in Illustration with a Fine Arts minor from the Art Institute of Boston. Her work has been featured in corporate communications and advertisements. To contact her, email: rachel.hirsh@verizon.net